Anne Boleyn

Henry VIII's Obsession

N

AMBERLEY

To my parents, Liss and Robin
With thanks to Hever Castle

This edition first published 2009

Amberley Publishing Plc
Cirencester Road, Chalford,
Stroud, Gloucestershire, GL6 8PE

www.amberley-books.com

Copyright © Elizabeth Norton, 2008, 2009

British Library Cataloguing in Publication Data.
A catalogue record for this book is available from the British Library.

ISBN 978 1 84868 514 7

Typesetting and Origination by Diagraf (www.diagraf.net)
Printed in Great Britain

Contents

Introduction

Anne Boleyn is the most controversial woman ever to wear the crown of England. Among Henry VIII's six wives, she is the only one to be a household name and she is remembered as both famous and infamous.

Even nearly five hundred years after her death, Anne still stirs up strong emotions. She often appears as a character in films, television and novels, as well as being the subject of numerous biographies. Accounts of Anne vary. Some biographers portray her as a victim of Henry VIII and an almost saintly figure, a woman who could do no wrong. Others portray Anne in a more hostile light, focussing on the rumours of murder and cruelty that surrounded her and on her treatment of Henry's first wife and eldest daughter. Anne Boleyn has been widely studied since at least the early nineteenth century. She remains as much a focus for debate as she was during her lifetime. Both today and in the sixteenth century people either loved or hated Anne Boleyn.

Anne Boleyn was no stereotype however. She was an extraordinary woman living in difficult times. In a world where noblewomen received arranged marriages, Anne forged her own path. She carved out a career for herself, first in Brussels and then in Paris before returning reluctantly for the marriage that was arranged for her. Anne rejected that marriage, a scandalous course for the time, and arranged her own much more high profile match. When this engagement was broken, Anne, who had little beauty, used her wit and grace to make herself one of the most talked about ladies of the court, even attracting the king.

Anne Boleyn is often portrayed as either a notorious woman or a saint. There is no doubt that she was driven by ambition and she did cause suffering to Henry's first wife, Catherine of Aragon, and her daughter, Mary, as well as to others who opposed her. However, Anne was not the wicked murderess portrayed in hostile sources, nor a monster. Equally, she was no Protestant saint, driven only by a desire for religious reform. Anne was ambitious and it was always her ambition that drove her.

Anne Boleyn was an exceptional woman for her day. She set out to arrange a grand marriage for herself and she can never have imagined just how great a marriage she could snare. When she saw a chance, she took it and she played the game as politically as any of Henry's ministers. In the end, Anne's gamble failed and she suffered for this as, ultimately, so too did many of the most prominent politicians of Henry's reign. Nobody would describe Thomas Cromwell or Cardinal Wolsey as helpless victims and Anne would also not have considered herself as a victim. She played the game and she lost, but she would have known that that was always a possibility. As Anne is frequently recorded as saying, there was a prophecy that a queen would be burned and she did not care. To become a queen, even with the risks associated with this, was a gamble worth taking.

Anne Boleyn was an extraordinary woman living in very difficult times for women. She did not set out to win the king and she may, at first, have been unsure of exactly what to do with the married Henry. She was unique and she fuelled a great love and lust in Henry which, in spite of his five other wives and numerous mistresses, he had never known before and would never know again. Only Anne Boleyn had the power to occupy Henry VIII's every waking thought and purpose. With her charm and her outspokenness, Anne was the most remarkable woman the king ever met. For nearly a decade she was always Henry VIII's passion and his obsession. It was that obsession that ultimately cost her her life as the reality of Anne, as wife and queen, could never live up to the image of her that had been built up in Henry's mind.

Anne Boleyn used Henry's obsession to drive him forward and change the course of English history over their marriage. Ultimately, however, Henry's obsessive love turned to hate and even Anne was unable to protect herself from the consequences.

CHAPTER 1

Sir Thomas Boleyn's Daughter

Anne Boleyn is usually considered an upstart, rising far above her station to grasp for the throne. This is the way she is perceived today and, to a certain extent, how she was perceived in her own time. However, although the Boleyns themselves were 'new money', Anne's ancestry was, for the most part, noble and, with the possible exception of Anne's first cousin, Catherine Howard, Anne was the most nobly born of Henry's English wives. She would certainly have considered herself far superior by birth to her successor, Jane Seymour.

Anne was the daughter of Sir Thomas Boleyn and his wife, Elizabeth Howard. The Boleyn family had risen to wealth and prominence during the lifetime of Anne's great-grandfather, Sir Geoffrey Boleyn. Geoffrey Boleyn was a merchant who rose to become Lord Mayor of London in 1457 and received a knighthood. By the time of his death in 1471 he was in a position to leave one thousand pounds to London charities, a vast sum at that time. He also purchased the great houses of Blickling Hall in Norfolk and Hever Castle in Kent.

If the Boleyn family originally came from humble origins, his newly acquired wealth allowed Geoffrey to arrange a good marriage for himself and an extremely advantageous match for his son. Geoffrey married well in choosing the daughter of Lord Hoo, and their son, Sir William Boleyn, made an even more advantageous match in marrying Margaret Butler, one of the two daughters and a co-heir of the Earl of Ormond. The Butlers were an ancient and noble family and Thomas Boleyn was a particular favourite of his grandfather, the Earl of Ormond. The earldom was also extremely wealthy and the Earl lived in England as an English peer. At the time of his death in 1515 Ormond left his daughters 72 manors in England alone, a vast inheritance. Thomas Boleyn placed himself firmly in the ranks of the nobility with his own marriage to Elizabeth Howard, daughter of the Earl of Surrey, and later the second Duke of Norfolk.

If the Boleyns still retained a slight stigma of new money by the turn of the sixteenth century, there was no such stigma about the Howards. The Duchy of Norfolk was one of the premier titles in England and the family could lay claim to royal blood through their descent from Edward I. Anne's uncle, the third Duke, also moved in royal circles through his marriage to Anne of York, daughter of Edward IV. Anne Boleyn's mother was therefore the sister of the brother-in-law of Henry VII and his queen, Elizabeth of York, a relatively close connection given the fact that Henry VII had no siblings of his own. Anne Boleyn's own uncle was therefore uncle by marriage to her future husband, Henry VIII.

Although Elizabeth Howard, with her impressive family connections, played a role in Anne's early life, it was Anne's father, Thomas Boleyn, who prepared her for a position of prominence in England. Elizabeth Howard is a shadowy figure who appears rarely in contemporary sources. She is so rarely mentioned that some confusion exists about her and a number of writers have claimed that she died in 1512 and that Thomas then remarried a woman of much lower rank. This could account for the little prominence given to Lady Boleyn during Anne's time as queen. However, it is not in fact the case. Anne's mother, Elizabeth Howard, survived her daughter, dying in 1538.

There is evidence that Elizabeth Howard served as a lady in waiting to Henry VIII's first wife, Catherine of Aragon, during the early years of Henry's reign. This is likely, given her family connections and the ambition of her husband, and it is about her time at court that the only stories surrounding Elizabeth Howard exist. Elizabeth Howard was one of the beauties of Henry's court and, according to a story surrounding her, she quickly attracted the attention of the much younger king. Henry VIII had led a closeted upbringing as Prince of Wales and it would therefore not be implausible that he was attracted to the older Elizabeth Howard; he was certainly attracted to Elizabeth's two daughters when they later arrived at his court. It is possible that Mary Boleyn resembled her mother and this may have been the source of Henry's attraction to Anne's sister. There were certainly rumours that Elizabeth Howard and Henry VIII had a relationship that was more than merely platonic. The Elizabethan writer, Sander, writing a report hostile to Anne went so far as to claim that 'Anne Boleyn was the daughter of Sir Thomas Boleyn's wife; I say his wife, because she could not have been the daughter of Sir Thomas, for she was born during his absence of two years in France on the king's affairs'. According to Sander, Thomas Boleyn demanded to know the father of the child. The king ordered Thomas to stop persecuting his wife and Thomas then 'learned from his wife that it was the king who had tempted her to sin, and that the child Anne was the daughter of no other than Henry VIII'. Sander claimed that Henry was fully aware that he was Anne's father and later paid for her to be educated in France.

Sander's account is clearly slander and it is impossible that Anne Boleyn could have been Henry VIII's daughter. Not only is there no evidence that Thomas Boleyn ever doubted her parentage but even the latest possible birth date for Anne is when Henry was only sixteen and still kept closely guarded by his over-protective father. It seems likely that the young king may have shown an interest in Elizabeth Howard during his early years on the throne but there is no evidence that she was ever his mistress. Rumours claiming that Anne was Henry's child did however circulate among their critics throughout their marriage and before.

There is no evidence that Anne was anything other than the daughter of Thomas Boleyn and, certainly, he was as ambitious for her as he was for all his children. As the grandson of the Earl of Ormond, Thomas could hardly be called an upstart and he continued to rise both in the service of Henry VII and Henry VIII. Thomas Boleyn was known to be the best French speaker at the Tudor court and was well educated. He was also highly intelligent and ambitious, traits that he passed on to his daughter. When Henry VIII came to the throne he promoted Thomas to the position of deputy-warden of the customs of Calais, making him a familiar face around court. This was a measure of Henry's confidence in Thomas Boleyn's abilities and he continued to be promoted steadily even before the rise of his daughter.

All three of Thomas Boleyn and Elizabeth Howard's surviving children were destined to come to prominence at the court of Henry VIII. However, the dates and even orders of the births of these children are nowhere recorded. Thomas Boleyn himself later complained that his wife had given birth to a child every year in their early marriage. This suggests that a number of children died in infancy and the couple's two eldest sons, Thomas and Henry, certainly died as babies.

Mary, Anne and George did however survive to adulthood and their ages and the orders of their births have been disputed for centuries.

The Elizabethan historian, William Camden, in his history of Anne's daughter, Elizabeth, claimed that Anne had been born in 1507. This was, until recently, generally accepted and the early seventeenth century account of the *Life of Jane Dormer*, which detailed the life of a lady-in-waiting to Anne's stepdaughter, Mary, supported this, stating that Anne 'was not twenty-nine years of age' at the time of her death. It has even been suggested that something about Anne's actual birth date can be calculated from the *Life of Jane Dormer* and that, to have not yet been 29 years old at the time of her death, she must have been born between 20 May and 31 December 1507.

A date of 1507 has long been accepted as Anne's birth date. However, it is clear from the evidence of Anne's life that this date is far too late. The author of the *Life of Jane Dormer* had read Camden's *History of Elizabeth* and the two dates therefore cannot be taken to be independent. Also, if Anne was born in 1507 then she would only have been six years old, at most, when she entered the household of Margaret of Austria and left England for the first time. This is simply implausible and, while princesses might be sent abroad in their infancy, the daughters of noblemen did not enter service at such an early age. A number of earlier dates have been suggested for Anne's birth and it will never be possible to say for certain when she was born. 1501 is commonly suggested however and this would seem to be the most likely date.

Anne's brother, George, was younger than her and would probably been born around 1504-1505. The order of seniority between Anne and her sister Mary has also been debated heavily and, once again, it is necessary to turn to the facts of their lives to form an opinion. It was Anne who was sent to Brussels in 1513 whilst Mary remained in England. This would seem to suggest that Anne was the elder sister. However, Mary was sent to France the following year and it is probable that Thomas Boleyn would have sent his more promising daughter to Margaret of Austria, rather than simply the eldest. Mary Boleyn also married for the first time on 4 February 1520. This suggests that Mary might have been the elder daughter as it would have been usual for the eldest daughter to marry first. Once again, it is not impossible that the younger daughter should have been married before the elder.

Better evidence for Mary Boleyn's seniority over Anne comes from a letter written by Mary's grandson, Lord Hunsdon, during the reign of Anne's daughter, Elizabeth. In this letter Lord Hunsdon claimed the Earldom of Ormond by virtue of his descent from the eldest daughter of Thomas Boleyn. In order to make his claim he set out a detailed, and convincing, family history. According to Lord Hunsdon:

'Sir Thomas Bullen was created Viscount Rocheforde and Erle of Ormonde to him and his heires generall, Erle of Wiltshire to him and his heires male, by whose death without issue male the Erldome of Wiltshire was extinguished, but the Erldome of Ormonde he surviving his other children before that time attainted, he in right leftе to his eldest daughter Marye, who had issue Henrye, and Henrye my selfe... Her Majesty is a cohcirc with me to the said Erledome viz: daughter and heire of Anne youngest daughter of the saide Sir Thomas Bullen late Erle of Ormonde... The saide dignitie of the Erledome of Ormonde together with his lands and mannors and tenements descended to my Grandmother his eldest daughter and sole heire and accordinglie she sued her liverie as by the recorde of the same doth and maie appeare. But admytt now as equallitie of desent then is it to be considered whether my Grandmother being the eldest daughter ought not to have the whole dignitie as in the Erldome of Chester'.

Lord Hunsdon's rather complicated account of the Boleyn titles shows that he had a good grasp of family history. Although his daughter, in her tomb memorial, stated that Mary Boleyn was the second daughter, it seems more likely that Lord Hunsdon was correct. Where the queen was his co-heir to the Boleyn title, he would have wanted to be very sure of his facts.

Mary Boleyn was probably born in either 1499 or 1500. Her birth was followed in around 1501 by Anne and a few years later the family was completed by the birth of George. Both Mary and Anne Boleyn were probably born at Blickling Hall in Norfolk although, at some point in their early childhood, the family moved to Hever Castle in Kent, the principal residence of the Boleyns. Mary Boleyn was the more conventionally attractive of the Boleyn sisters and, at the time of her birth, Anne may have seemed particularly unpromising. Much has been written about whether or not Anne Boleyn was born with physical deformities which, in a superstitious age, would have been taken to denote witchcraft or the mark of the devil. These include a sixth finger on one hand and a large mole on her neck, both of which she took trouble to hide. These deformities do not appear in her portraits but, then, they would not be expected to do so. It seems unlikely that Anne suffered from as many deformities as some hostile sources suggest but it is just possible that she had the beginning of a sixth finger on one of her hands. Certainly, this claim has been particularly persistent and even Anne's supporter, George Wyatt, in his *Life of Queen Anne* claimed that:

'There was found, indeed, upon the side of her nail upon one of her fingers, some little show of a nail, which yet was so small, by the report of those that have seen her, as the workmaster seemed to leave it as occasion of greater grace to her hand, which, with the tips of one of her other fingers, might be and was usually by her hidden without any least blemish to it'.

This was certainly not a full sixth finger which later writers have suggested but it may have been the subject of a few worried glances when Anne was born and during her childhood. George Wyatt also claimed that Anne had some minor blemishes and that 'likewise there were said to be upon some parts of her body certain small moles incident to the clearest complexions'. This was very far from being a large and disfiguring mole on her neck however and it is probable that Anne's blemishes and sixth nail merely ensured that Mary was the beauty of the Boleyn family rather than Anne. In any event, Anne's dark colouring, which she apparently inherited from her father, made her very far from a conventional beauty in the early sixteenth century.

In spite of her lack of conventional beauty, Sir Thomas Boleyn recognised his younger daughter's promise from an early age and he ensured that Anne received a good education during her early childhood. No details survive of Anne's childhood at either Blickling or Hever. Given her parents' duties at court, they were probably distant figures and Anne and her siblings would have been raised by members of their parents' household. They are likely to have remained in the country for the majority of their time and they would have socialised with neighbours, such as the Wyatt family, who lived close to Hever. The Wyatts' eldest son, Thomas, was a similar age to Anne and there may have been a friendship between them during Anne's early childhood. However, most of Anne's time would have been spent with her sister and her brother and there was a particular closeness between Anne and George which would survive into adulthood. The three probably shared the same tutors and both Anne and George excelled at their lessons, setting them apart a little from the elder Mary.

As well as receiving a good education, Anne would also have been taught more traditional feminine accomplishments such as singing, dancing, music and needlework. Anne would have been aware that these were skills necessary to show her to the best advantage when she came to look for a husband.

Thomas Boleyn, although a distant figure to his children, was an extremely ambitious man. He used his children to further his ambition throughout their lives, something that also worked to Anne's advantage. Thomas Boleyn's intelligence and ambition was also recognised by both Henry VII and Henry VIII and he was appointed as an esquire of the body to both kings in turn. He was also created a Knight of the Bath at Henry VIII's coronation and would have been regularly present at court during the early years of Henry's reign. Despite his frequent and prolonged absences from home, he would have been an all-important figure to Anne and her siblings during their childhood. While no details of Anne before 1513 survive she would have tried hard to please him.

Anne certainly appears to have outstripped Mary in her education and she quickly became the focus of Thomas Boleyn's ambition for his daughters. The Boleyns had risen through making advantageous marriages and both Mary and Anne would have been aware that they were expected to attract prominent husbands. Thomas Boleyn was often employed by the king on diplomatic missions and it was during one such mission that he managed to arrange a placement for Anne that would provide her with an extra advantage in the marriage market. In 1513 Anne's childhood formally ended and she was sent by her father to Brussels to serve at one of the most accomplished courts in Europe: the court of Margaret of Austria, regent of the Netherlands. The fact that it was Anne, rather than the older Mary, who was sent indicates Thomas Boleyn's confidence in his daughter and his hopes for the fine marriage she would make in the future. For all her physical imperfections and lack of conventional beauty, Anne stood out for her intelligence and her father was determined that she should be displayed at her best when the time came for her to take a husband.

CHAPTER 2

So Pleasing in Her Youthful Age

Anne would have felt a mixture of apprehension and excitement as she left England for the first time in the summer of 1513. She was proud that she had been selected to become one of Margaret of Austria's ladies but also anxious as she set out, accompanied by a small group of her father's servants. At twelve years old, Anne would have known that her childhood was over and that she was being given an opportunity to launch herself into an adult world far superior to that offered to most girls of her age. Anne knew that she was expected to improve herself as well as be a representative of the Boleyn family and she would have been instructed by her father in how to behave.

An appointment as one of the maids of Margaret of Austria was greatly sought after and Anne was drilled by her father in how fortunate she was to achieve such a position. It was a mark of Margaret's affection for Thomas that she agreed to take his daughter and it is clear that Thomas had confidence in Anne's abilities to impress. Margaret of Austria headed one of the most cultured courts in Europe and, as the first court that Anne would have visited, she must have felt a sense of awe when she arrived in Brussels.

Margaret of Austria was the only daughter of the Emperor Maximilian I and Mary of Burgundy and, as a child, she was sent to France to be raised as the betrothed wife of Charles IX. However, after several years in France Margaret suffered a humiliation when Charles married the heiress to Brittany instead. Margaret must have been distraught to be rejected by the man she considered herself to be married to and she would have returned in shame to her father. A new marriage was quickly arranged for her and she was sent to Spain to marry the young heir of Isabella and Ferdinand of Spain before being widowed equally quickly. Margaret's third and final marriage was also short and by 1513 she was determined to reject any further marriages, having had three unhappy experiences. By 1513, she was also one of the most powerful women in Europe and had little need of a husband to maintain her position.

Following the death of Margaret's brother, Philip, she had been appointed regent of the Netherlands and guardian of Philip's young son, the future Emperor Charles V. Margaret was passionately loyal to the Netherlands, which her brother had inherited from their mother, and one of her most cherished beliefs was the need for an alliance with England. In one letter that she wrote to her father, for example, she pointed out that 'between the Catholic king (Ferdinand of Spain) and France there are great mountains, and between France and England there is the sea, but between his (Charles V's) lands and France there is no separation, and you know the great and inveterate hatred which the French bear to this house'. Margaret believed that this alliance could be best maintained through the marriage of her nephew Charles to Mary Tudor, the sister of Henry VIII, and she worked hard to ensure that it could be achieved. It is possible that Margaret particularly sought out Anne on her arrival in order to learn something of the language and the customs familiar to Mary Tudor.

Anne would have been relieved at the attention that Margaret showed her on her arrival and she quickly settled into her duties. She was anxious to please and made such a favourable impression on the Regent that Margaret wrote personally to Thomas praising his clever young daughter:

'I have received your letter by the Esquire Bouton, who presented to me your daughter, who was very welcome to me, and I hope to treat her in such a fashion that you will have reason to be content with it; at least be sure that until your return there need be no other intermediary between you and me than she; and I find her of such good address and so pleasing in her youthful age that I am more beholden to you for having sent her to me than you are to me'.

This letter demonstrates the remarkable regard in which Margaret held Thomas Boleyn and also the favour she showed his daughter. It is a mark of Anne's intelligence that she made such a good impression so quickly and Thomas Boleyn must have felt that this letter confirmed his choice of Anne over her sister.

Thomas Boleyn was an excellent French speaker and Anne inherited his talent for languages. Although she knew little, if any, French before she left England she quickly picked up the language. Her first surviving letter, written to her father in the curious French of a beginner, shows the progress she had made in only a few short weeks. The fact that Thomas Boleyn preserved this letter amongst his papers until his death demonstrates just how proud he was of his daughter and of the impression she made in Brussels. The letter, as the first time that Anne's voice is apparent in the sources, is useful to quote in full:

'Sir, - I understand by your letter that you desire that I shall be a worthy woman when I come to the Court and you inform me that the queen will take the trouble to converse with me, which rejoices me much to think of talking with a person so wise and worthy. This will make me have greater desire to continue to speak French well and also spell especially because you have so enjoined it on me, and with my own hand I inform you that I will observe it the best I can. Sir, I beg you to excuse me if my letter is badly written, for I assure you that the orthography is from my own understanding alone, while the others were only written by my hand, and Semmonet tells me the letter but wants so that I may do it myself, for fear that it shall not be known unless I acquaint you, and I pray you that the light of [?] may not be allowed to drive away the will which you say you have to help me, for it seems to me that you are sure [?] you can, if you please, make me a declaration of your word, and concerning me be certain that there shall be neither [?] nor ingratitude which might check or efface my affection, which is determined to [?] as much unless it shall please you to order me, and I promise you that my love is based on such great strength that it will never grow less, and I will make an end to my [?] after having commended myself right humbly to your good grace. Written at [?Veure] by your very humble and very obedient daughter, Anna de Boullan'.

Anne's French is eccentric and it is not always possible to understand what she meant to say but the length and content of the letter shows the progress she had made in the language and her enjoyment of her time at Brussels. She learned French quickly, as her father had hoped she would, and by 1514 it is clear that word had reached the English court of her fluency in the language.

When Anne arrived in Brussels in 1513, England was firmly allied with Spain and the Habsburg Empire against France. Both Maximilian and Ferdinand of Aragon had a common interest in their grandson, and common heir, the future Charles V. Charles was the son of Maximilian's deceased eldest son Philip and Ferdinand's eldest surviving daughter, Juana, Queen of Castile. Juana, although Queen of Castile in her own right through her mother, Isabella, had, by 1513, spent several years imprisoned on the grounds of insanity while her father ruled her kingdom on her behalf. Henry VIII, through his marriage to Catherine of Aragon the daughter of Ferdinand, naturally allied himself to their interests and, in 1511, had sent troops to aid Ferdinand in his war with France. In 1513 Henry joined the war personally and sailed to France with an army, besieging and winning two French cities. This was Henry's first taste of war and he 'returned to England back again with triumph and glory'. News of the victories would also have been celebrated at Margaret's court and Anne would have been pleased with the continuing alliance between Margaret and her own country. Anne may also have been given the opportunity to meet Henry VIII for the first time when Margaret, Maximilian and Henry met at Lille during the war in late August 1513, although Anne's presence is nowhere recorded at the meeting.

The betrothal between Margaret's nephew and Mary Tudor had been agreed during the lifetimes of the couple's fathers and Mary was always known in England as the Princess of Castile. Charles, as the heir to Spain, the Habsburg Empire and the Netherlands, was the greatest marriage prospect in Europe and Henry VIII was anxious for the marriage to be concluded as soon as he returned from France. According to Hall's Chronicle he quickly set about making preparations to send Mary to Brussels when he received word from Margaret's council that, while they would happily receive Mary Tudor in the Netherlands, they could not provide a dower for her without the further agreement of Ferdinand of Aragon. This was certainly a delaying tactic as 'the kynge lyke a lovynge brother would not sende his syster wyldely without a dowar'.

Margaret was as dismayed and angry as Henry when she was told that Charles's marriage to Mary Tudor could not take place in 1513 and she wrote to her father strongly urging him to continue in his alliance with England. Maximilian however refused to allow her to arrange the marriage and the following year, when Henry again attempted to send Mary to the Netherlands he was once again rebuffed. For Henry, this was the final straw and he began to look around for a new marriage for his sister and a new alliance. Ferdinand of Aragon had made a separate truce with France in April 1513 and by the spring of 1514 Maximilian was also considering a French alliance. Henry also decided on a French alliance, in spite of Margaret of Austria's attempts to keep the English alliance in place.

Anne of Brittany, the woman who had supplanted Margaret as queen of France, died in January 1514, leaving her second husband, Louis XII of France a widower. Anne of Brittany bore her husband only two daughters and the aged Louis needed to remarry to secure the succession for his own son, rather than his son-in-law, Francis of Angouleme. There were rumours that Louis would seek to marry Margaret of Austria herself but, instead, perceiving the breakdown of Henry's Habsburg alliance, Louis asked the English king for the hand of his sister. The marriage was quickly arranged, in spite of the thirty year age gap between the two parties, much to the dismay of Margaret of Austria. The marriage also had a profound effect on Anne Boleyn.

Word of Anne's fluency in French had reached the English court by the time Mary Tudor's French marriage was arranged and Thomas Boleyn was asked to recall his daughter so that she could go to France to serve the new French queen. Given the warm relationship between Thomas and Margaret, this was probably very far from his wishes for his daughter but he had no choice but to comply and wrote in 1514 requesting that Margaret release Anne from her household. Anne would have been dismayed to leave the most cultured court in Europe. She may also have borne the brunt of Margaret's anger at the English alliance with France and the breaking of Charles's betrothal. Certainly, news of Mary Tudor's new betrothal was greeted with bitterness in the Netherlands. According to Hall's Chronicle, 'the Dutchmen heryng these newes were sory, and repented then that they receyved not the lady, and spake shamefully of this marriage, that a feble old & pocky man should mary so fayre a lady'. Margaret of Austria probably shared these sentiments and Anne's last weeks in Brussels may have been uncomfortable. There was no time for her to return to England and she travelled directly to France to meet Mary Tudor. Anne had already spent over a year away from her home and it would have been a much more confident Anne who joined Mary Tudor at some point during the new French queen's early days in France. Anne would also have been reunited with her sister, Mary, who had secured a place in Mary Tudor's household and travelled with her from England.

If Margaret of Austria had been angered by news of Mary Tudor's betrothal to Louis XII, the bride herself was completely dismayed. Louis XII was in his fifties and had long suffered from ill health, including gout. Mary Tudor on the other hand was only in her late teens and was renowned as the most beautiful princess in Europe. As the youngest of Henry VII and Elizabeth of York's surviving children, Mary had always been spoiled by her brother and she had developed an independence unusual in a princess of her time. When she was told by her brother of the marriage he had arranged for her, she refused it. Finally, she and Henry reached a compromise of which she reminded him later:

'For the good of peace and for the furtherance of your affairs you moved me to marry with my lord and late husband, King Louis of France, whose soul God pardon. Though I understood that he was very aged and sickly, yet for the advancement of the said peace, and for the furtherance of your causes, I was contented to conform myself to your said motion, so that if I should fortune to survive the said late king I might with your good will marry myself at my liberty without your displeasure. Whereunto, good brother, you condescended and granted, as you well know, promising unto me that in such case you would never provoke or move me but as mine own heart and mind should be best pleased; and that wheresoever I should dispose myself, you would wholly be contented with the same. And upon that, your good comfort and faithful promise, I assented to the said marriage, which else I would never have granted to, as at the same time I shewed unto you more at large'.

Henry would probably have said anything to ensure that his sister agreed to the marriage and he repeated his promise to Mary on the beach at Dover before she sailed for France. Mary Boleyn, who was waiting with Mary Tudor's other attendants, may well have witnessed the princess's distress as she took her leave of her brother at Dover on 2 October 1514 and she would have reported this to her sister when they were together in France.

It is unclear when Anne joined Mary Tudor in France. She may perhaps have been present at Mary's marriage on 9 October in the cathedral at Abbeville. Her absence from a list of ladies retained by Louis XII to serve his wife suggests that she had not yet joined the French queen at the time of the marriage and she may have been retained by an angry Margaret of Austria. If this was the case, she missed the major trauma in Mary Tudor's household when her husband sent all but a few of her English ladies home to England. While this was a trauma for Mary Tudor, the fact that both Mary and

Anne Boleyn were amongst the few English ladies remaining with the French queen was advantageous to them and they would have found themselves often in close proximity to the queen.

In spite of her distaste for her elderly husband, Mary Tudor quickly settled into married life with Louis and she was an exemplary wife towards him. The great contrast between the aged king and his lively wife did however continue to cause controversy and it is possible that there were some rumours surrounding Mary Tudor's behaviour. According to the sixteenth century writer, the Seigneur de Brantome, Mary's relationship with the husband of her stepdaughter, Francis of Angouleme, caused particular comment. According to Brantome, Mary and Francis quickly fell in love with each other and they were close to consummating their relationship when Monsieur De Grignaux, a member of the court, noticed what was happening. According to Brantome, M. De Grignaux recognised the danger that Francis was in from the predatory Mary and warned him saying:

'"What would you be at? See you not this woman, keen and cunning as she is, is fain to draw you to her, to the end you may get her with child? But an if she come to have a son, what of you? You are still plain Comte d'Angouleme, and never king of France, as you hope to be'.

Francis was attracted to Mary and it is possible that she may have shared something of this. However, she had very little time to even consider being unfaithful to Louis and she and her ladies lived quietly in Paris during her brief time as queen. Louis XII had been rejuvenated by his marriage to Mary, but it was a temporary recovery and, on 1 January 1515, he died after less than three months of marriage. Mary Tudor apparently fainted on hearing the news of her husband's death.

As the widow of a king who had no sons, Mary Tudor was expected to spend time in mourning and seclusion whilst it was established that there was no possibility that she would bear the king a posthumous son. Anne Boleyn, as one of Mary's attendants, shared in her mistress's mourning and she retired with the French Queen to the palace of Cluny. Anne would have braced herself for a number of boring months in seclusion and it is unlikely that she, or any of Mary Tudor's other attendants, had any idea of the dramatic events that would take place whilst Mary was supposed to be mourning for her husband.

When Mary Tudor had stood on the beach at Dover and begged her brother to remember his promise to her she already had her second husband in mind. Charles Brandon had been a childhood companion of Henry VIII and the king had created him Duke of Suffolk. Mary Tudor and Suffolk were attracted to each other in England and Mary later wrote to her brother describing Suffolk as one 'to whom I have always been of good mind, as well you know'. Henry did indeed know of his sister's affection for his friend and before sending him to France Henry insisted that Suffolk promised that he would not seek to marry Mary. Henry was satisfied with this promise and Suffolk arrived in France soon after Louis XII's death in order to bring Mary home to England.

Anne and the other ladies were probably glad of the interruption to their seclusion afforded by the appearance of the English lords. For Mary Tudor, Suffolk's arrival heralded a way out of her predicament. Francis of Angouleme, now Francis I of France, had been showing Mary unwanted attentions of which Anne and the other ladies would have been aware and alarmed. According to a letter sent by Mary to her brother:

'Pleaseth it your grace, the French [king] on Tuesday night last [past], came to visit me, and [had] with me many diverse [discoursin]g, among the which he demanded me whether I had [ever] made any promise of marriage in any place, assuring me upon his honour, and upon the word of a prince, that in case I would be plain [with] him in that affair, he would do for me therein to the best of his power, whether it were in his realm or out of the same. Whereunto I answered, that I would disclose unto him the secret of my heart in hu[mili]ty, as unto the prince of the world after your grace in whom I had m[ost trust], and so declar[ed] unto him the good mind [which] for divers consi[derations I] bear to my lord of Suffolk, asking him not only [to grant] me his favour and consent thereunto, but [also] that he would of his [own] hand write unto your grace, and pray you to bear your like favour unto me, and to be content with the same; the which he granted me to do, and so hath done, according as shall appear unto your grace by his said [letters]'.

Mary begged her brother to agree to the marriage saying that she only told Francis this because of 'the extreme pain and annoyance I was i[n, by reason] of such suit as t[he French kin]g made unt[o me not accord]ing with mine honour'. Mary Tudor was in an agony of confusion as she stayed at Cluny, something that must have been witnessed by her ladies as she attempted to fend off the married Francis's advances towards her.

Like Suffolk, Mary had assured her brother that she would make no promise of marriage before she returned to England. However, when Suffolk arrived in France Francis gave him an audience, telling him that he knew that he had come to marry Mary. Suffolk tried to protest that this was not the case but Francis ignored him, promising to help him arrange the marriage. Francis had also been putting pressure on Mary and, in terror, she had come to believe that she would be married to Charles V if she returned unmarried to England. When Suffolk went to see Mary he found her in a distressed state and, according to his own account she 'would never let me [be] in rest till I had granted her to be married, and so, to be plain with you, I have married her harettylle [heartily] and has lyen wyet her, in soo moche [as] I fyer me lyes that sche by wyet chyld'.

Henry VIII was furious when he heard of his sister's marriage, but the couple had presented him with a *fait accompli* and there was little he could do. The couple returned to Dover on 2 May 1515 and were publicly married later in the month at Greenwich. For Mary Tudor and most of her ladies, the marriage signalled the end of their time in France. Anne Boleyn did not return with her mistress and, presumably using her language skills and other accomplishments, quickly secured a place for herself at the French court in the household of the new queen of France.

CHAPTER 3

Mademoiselle Boleyn

Anne and Mary Boleyn entered the household of Queen Claude upon Mary Tudor's return to England. Anne was to remain with Claude for seven years and the French queen must have developed a fondness for her. It seems likely that Anne would have been called upon to act as an interpreter between Mary Tudor and her stepdaughter, Claude, and this may be how Anne first came into contact with her.

Claude was fifteen when her father, Louis XII, died and her husband, Francis I, came to the throne. Due to the Salic Law in operation in France, Claude, as a woman, was barred from inheriting the crown but she was Duchess of Brittany in her own right following the death of her mother. Although treated respectfully by Francis I and his court, Claude was overshadowed by Francis's mother, Louise of Savoy, and his sister, Marguerite of Angouleme. She also suffered yearly pregnancies and died young. Such was her piety, that there were suggestions that Claude should be canonised after her death. Given the fact that Anne Boleyn stayed with Claude for seven years she must have had some regard for her. Claude's rather staid household was tedious for the lively Boleyn sisters and both would have been glad on the rare occasions when Claude's household joined the main French court.

Francis I was only in his early twenties when he came to the throne and his court was very different from that of his pious wife. Francis had married Claude at her father's request and also for her position as heiress of Brittany. While he always showed her the utmost respect in public she was certainly not often in his thoughts and Francis's court was renowned for its licentiousness. Chasing women was one of Francis I's chief pastimes and, according to a near contemporary, the

Seigneur de Brantome, Francis said that the best way to please him was:

> 'By offering to his view on his first arrival a beautiful woman, a fine horse and a handsome hound. For by casting his gaze now on the one, now on the other and presently on the third, he would never be a-weary in that house, having there the three things most pleasant to look upon and admire, and so exercising his eyes right agreeably'.

Following Francis's accession to the crown the ladies of his court quickly gained something of a reputation with reports that 'the ladies thereof, both maids and wives, do oft-times trip, indeed do so customarily'. Brantome considered this rumour to be false and that the French ladies were, in fact, honourable and virtuous. He also said that the liberty accorded to ladies in France served only to make them 'more desirable and loveable, more easy of access and more amenable, than they of any other nation'. Both Anne and Mary Boleyn would have enjoyed the freedom afforded to them as members of the court of France. Mary Boleyn however appears to have taken this freedom a little too far.

The Elizabethan writer Sander, in an account hostile to Anne claimed that at the French court she was known as 'the English mare, because of her shameless behaviour; and then the royal mule. When she became acquainted with the King of France'. Sander believed that Anne had disgraced herself in France by indulging first in sexual relations with members of Francis's court and later with Francis himself. According to his account, even in the notoriously licentious French court, Anne Boleyn stood out for her immorality. It is clear that Sander has confused the two sisters in his account and that it was in fact Mary Boleyn who attained the reputation of both the 'English mare' and the 'royal mule'.

Mary Boleyn became the mistress of Francis I soon after his accession. This was only a casual affair and certainly not as lasting as the affair that Mary would later enjoy with Henry VIII in England. Francis quickly tired of Mary and she then became the mistress of other French courtiers. Mary Boleyn quickly obtained a notorious reputation helped in no small part by Francis's own view of her. Years later he would refer to her as a great prostitute and infamous above all. Anne must have been horrified at Mary for throwing herself away so cheaply. Mary Boleyn received no tangible benefits for the loss of her honour and her conduct horrified her family in England. Mary was quickly sent for by her parents and returned home to England to avoid any further scandal. Anne may have been relieved that her sister was no longer in a position at court to disgrace her further. There is certainly no evidence of closeness between the two sisters and Anne often felt that she had cause for embarrassment due to Mary's behaviour.

Following Mary Boleyn's disgrace, Anne may have been glad of the relative seclusion of Claude's household. Claude was often in ill health and lived quietly away from court. During the times that Claude's household was separate from the king's Anne would have spent much of her time at her needlework. She could also play the lute, sing and dance and she may have been expected to help entertain the queen. Anne probably also took part in Claude's coronation in May 1516 at St Denis and the queen's state entry to Paris. These were grand state occasions which Anne would have enjoyed. She appears also to have met Francis's sister, the accomplished Marguerite of Angouleme. Marguerite later became known for her reformist views and Anne may, perhaps, have first become exposed to these ideas through her proximity to Marguerite. It has been suggested by one critical writer that it was while she was in France that Anne first 'embraced the heresy of Luther'.

Anne would also have had a number of opportunities to see her father whilst she was in France. Thomas Boleyn had continued to rise in prominence during Anne's absence from England and was frequently sent on missions to France. In early 1519, for example, Thomas was part of a mission to France headed by the Bishop of Ely and the Earl of Worcester. This mission coincided with the birth of Claude's son Henry, Duke of Orleans, and Thomas Boleyn is known to have attended the christening. Anne must have enjoyed seeing her father on his visits and he was probably pleased with the way that her education and deportment had progressed during his absences. Anne would also have had the opportunity to see Thomas and several other members of her family at the major event of the early years of Francis's reign, the Field of the Cloth of Gold.

In October 1518 Francis concluded a treaty of perpetual friendship with Henry VIII which included a marriage alliance between Francis's infant son, the Dauphin Francis, and Henry's daughter, Mary. As part of this treaty it was agreed that the two kings would meet for the first time, something that both kings were eager to do. Both kings were of a similar age and they were fascinated by each other. One account, written just after Francis's accession to the throne, shows just how anxious Henry was to ensure that he was the superior of the two kings. According to the account:

'His Majesty [Henry] came into our arbour, and addressing me in French, said "Talk with me awhile! The King of France, is he as tall as I am?" I told him there was but little difference. He continued, "Is he as stout?" I said he was not, and he then inquired "What sort of leg has he?" I replied "Spare". Whereupon he opened the front of his doublet, "look here! And I have also a good calf to my leg"'.

Francis was as eager as Henry to impress and he would have been long used to hearing reports of Henry's handsomeness and his athletic prowess. According to one writer, who saw Henry in 1515:

'His Majesty [Henry] is the handsomest potentate I ever set eyes on; above the usual height, with an extremely fine calf to his leg, his complexion very fair and bright, with auburn hair combed straight and short, in the French fashion, and a round face so very beautiful, that it would become a pretty woman, his throat being rather long and thick'.

Henry cut a very impressive figure. He could speak French and Latin fluently, as well as a little Italian. He could also play the lute and harpsichord and sing from a book at sight, as well as being an athlete with a bow or at jousting. Both kings were determined to outshine the other at their meeting in France between 7 June and 20 June 1520. The meeting was so renowned for its splendour that it has always been known as the Field of the Cloth of Gold.

Anne Boleyn is not recorded at the Field of the Cloth of Gold but she was almost certainly present. As one of Claude's ladies, Anne's presence would have been required and her ability to act as an interpreter would also have been in demand. Anne prepared for the meeting with excitement, both for the spectacle and for the chance to see family and friends from England again. The French party were scheduled to stay at Ardres, a town near the English possession of Calais, and Claude and her ladies began their slow progress towards the town in April. Claude's household reached Paris on 5 May and was joined there by Francis on 17 May. The court as a whole then moved on to Abbeville and then towards Ardres, arriving there on 31 May. The French were represented by over 6,000 people and they must have waited expectantly for word that the 5,172 Englishmen and women had arrived at the English camp at nearby Guisnes.

The two kings finally met on 7 June about one mile outside Guisnes. Although the meeting had been arranged to be a friendly one there must have been a certain amount of tension and both kings had agreed to be, effectively, hostages for the other. According to one source, the two kings rode out to meet each other and immediately dismounted and embraced as a sign of their friendship. The initial meeting was a success and the two kings retired to a tent made of cloth of gold to speak with each other. Anne Boleyn may have been among the crowds and, if so, this was perhaps her first sight of Henry VIII. Henry was then still only thirty and, like everyone else, she must have been in awe of him.

If Anne was not present on 7 June then she would certainly have been present on 11 June on the opening day of the jousts. A gallery had been built for the two queens beside the tiltyard to allow them to watch the tournament. Catherine of Aragon and her sister-in-law, Mary Tudor, arrived in litters, Mary Tudor's bearing the emblems and initials of her late husband, Louis XII of France. Catherine and Mary also brought a large retinue of ladies with them either riding in three wagons covered in cloth of gold or riding on horses. Anne would have been amongst Claude's ladies and followed her mistress, perhaps riding in one of the three wagons covered in cloth of silver. This would have been the first time that Anne was to see Catherine of Aragon and she may have felt that the queen, who was in her mid-thirties, was a poor match for her glamorous husband.

The jousts continued throughout the week with both Henry and Francis taking part. Anne's services would have been constantly in demand as an interpreter and she must have enjoyed the opportunity to reacquaint herself with her family. She may also have been present on 13 June when the kings arrived to find that it was too windy for the jousts to take place. Henry asked to wrestle with Francis, aware that he was the larger man. It is probable that Henry expected to easily beat the French king and he was highly embarrassed when Francis threw him to the ground. This cast a shadow over the proceedings for Henry but the jousts continued on 14 June, as did other festivities.

The Field of the Cloth of Gold was intended to be a period of great festivities and a number of banquets were also held to demonstrate the friendship between the two countries and their kings. On 11 June it was arranged that Francis would dine at Guisnes with Catherine, and Henry would dine with Claude at Ardres. Shots were fired at exactly the same time from Guisnes and Ardres to indicate that the two kings had set out and the queens and their ladies must have waited with anticipation for the arrival of their guests. Anne would have remained with Claude to await the arrival of the English king. Both banquets were a success and Henry dined with Claude before dancing with her ladies. The French queen and her ladies also displayed the wealth of France with Claude dressed in cloth of gold embroidered with jewels and with a large diamond on her breast. At the English camp Francis, true to his reputation, also set out to charm the English ladies and 'went from one ende of the Chamber to thither on both sides and with his capp in his hand and kissed that ladies and gentilweomen one after another saving iii or five that were ould and not faire standing together'.

Both banquets were a great success and Henry once again dined with Claude and Francis with Catherine on 17 June. Henry dined privately with Claude before secretly dressing for a masque with a number of the men who accompanied him. Some of the lords wore old fashioned gowns of blue satin:

'Then was there another compaignie of X lords in whiche maskery the king was himself, apparelled all in long garments of estate all pale riche clothe of golde, all these had riche gounes which were lined with grene taffeta, and knit with pointes of Venice silver wherewith the riche clothe together was fastened on their faces cisers, and all the berdes were fine wyre of Duchet gold'.

Henry had also brought a troupe of minstrels with him to play as he and his company passed through the streets of Ardres. They came into the presence of Claude and danced with the French ladies. When Claude gave the signal, the masquers removed their masks to show their faces to the ladies with whom they had been dancing. Anne Boleyn would certainly have been one of the ladies present and she would have danced with the Englishmen. She must have been thrilled by the whole performance and it would have been an evening she remembered all her life. It is impossible to say who Anne danced with but it is not impossible that she may have danced with Henry as an Englishwoman present at the French court. She would have been called on to interpret during the evening and this would have given her a prominence. Even if Henry did not notice Anne, she would certainly have noticed him and been impressed by him.

Anne was probably also in attendance at mass on 23 June when a temporary chapel had been set up overnight on the site of the tournament. This was the first time that she saw Henry VIII's chief minister, Cardinal Wolsey, and he would have been an impressive figure as he said mass to the congregation. Anne, like everyone else assembled, must have been looking forward to the banquet that was to be held that evening. Henry once again dined with Claude, arriving dressed in costume for a masque on the life of Hercules. The two kings met on their way home from the feasts and embraced each other, signifying the end of the celebration.

The two weeks of the Field of the Cloth of Gold must have been amongst the most memorable of Anne's life and the splendour of the festival certainly remained in the minds of all those who witnessed them. John Fisher, Bishop of Rochester, mused on the meeting following the English party's return to England and provided a useful summary of just what it meant to those who witnessed the spectacle. Bishop Fisher commented that three queens had been present (Catherine of Aragon, Claude and Mary Tudor) and that:

'Euery of them accompanied with so many of other fayre ladyes in sumptuous and gorgeous apparell, suche daunsynges, suche armonyes, suche dalyaunce, and so many pleasaunt pastimes, so curious howses and buyldynges, so preciously apparayled, suche costely welfare of dyners, soppers, and bankettys, so delycate wynes, soo precyouse meatys, suche and soo many noble men of armes, soo ryche and goodly tentys, suche justynges, suche tourneys, and suche feates of warre. These assuredly were wonderfull syghtes as for this worlde'.

The Field of the Cloth of Gold caught the imaginations of everyone who was present and Anne would have been no exception. She may have watched the queens and felt envious of their positions. It was the greatest event in which she took part during her time in France. By the time of the Field of the Cloth of Gold Anne had lived in France for six years and she must have felt wholly French. The meeting with the English ladies emphasised just how different she was with her French upbringing. Anne would probably have been content to remain in France for the rest of her life. However, by late 1521 she would have known that this was not an option and her father was actively pushing for her return to England. Anne delayed her return for as long as possible but by the time she sailed for England in early 1522 she knew that her future lay in England, not in France.

CHAPTER 4

A Secret Love

Anne Boleyn returned to England in early 1522 after nearly nine years away. She would have had little time to reacquaint herself with her family and the familiar places of her childhood because, by February or March at latest, Anne had joined the household of Catherine of Aragon at Greenwich. Anne would have found the English court very different to the court of France and she may well have been disappointed with what she found there. It was a very different world that Anne entered in early 1522 and she, being French in all but birth, was also a very different person to the young girl who had left for the continent nearly a decade before.

Anne immediately caused a stir at court, in spite of her lack of conventional beauty. According to her biographer, George Wyatt:

> 'There was at this present, presented to the eye of the court the rare and admirable beauty of the fresh and young Lady Anne Bolengne, to be attending upon the queen. In this noble imp, the graces of nature graced by gracious education, seemed even at the first to have promised bliss unto her aftertimes. She was taken at that time to have a beauty not so whitely as clear and fresh above all we may esteem, which appeared much more excellent by her favour passing sweet and cheerful, and these, both also increased by her noble presence of shape and fashion, representing both mildness and majesty more than can be expressed'.

At a time when the ideal of beauty was blond hair and a pink complexion, Anne's dark hair and skin did not make her a beauty. However, there was something more to Anne Boleyn and even sources hostile to her suggest that she had something else which marked her out at court as one of the stars. The hostile Sander, for example, writing in the reign of Anne's daughter, Elizabeth, claimed that Anne:

> 'Was rather tall of stature, with black hair, and an oval face of a sallow complexion, as if troubled with jaundice. She had a projecting tooth under the upper lip, and on her right hand six fingers. There was a large wen under her chin, and therefore to hide its ugliness she wore a high dress covering her throat. In this she was followed by the ladies of the court, who also wore high dresses having before been in the habit of leaving their necks and the upper portion of their persons uncovered. She was handsome to look at, with a pretty mouth, amusing in her ways, playing well on the lute, and was a good dancer. She was the model and mirror of those who were at court. For she was always well dressed, and every day made some change in the fashion of her garments'.

Even Sander, who clearly despised Anne and could not resist providing an almost comical picture of her extreme ugliness, admitted that there was something unusual about her. While it is not impossible that Anne may have had the beginnings of a rudimentary sixth finger on her right hand, it seems very unlikely that she would have attracted as much favourable attention as she did if she had possessed the other defects claimed by Sander. Sander himself also, perhaps unwittingly, demonstrates something of the nature of Anne Boleyn. Although no beauty by contemporary standards, she possessed a grace and self-possession admired by both men and women alike. Men were fascinated by Anne for her grace and poise and women sought to emulate her in her clothing and manner. Anne Boleyn was a leader of fashion and quickly became a star at the court of Henry VIII.

In March 1522, probably only weeks after her arrival at Greenwich, Anne was chosen to take part in the masque which followed a great banquet at court. This was a singular honour and shows how quickly Anne was able to captivate much of the court. For the masque, a castle had been built in one of the rooms of Greenwich palace. At the top of this castle stood eight ladies wearing gowns of white satin and caps of gold and jewels. The eight ladies represented Beauty, Honour, Perseverance, Kindness, Constance, Bounty, Mercy and Pity. Henry's sister, Mary, the French Queen, played the part of Beauty. Anne's sister, Mary, took the role of Kindness and even George Boleyn's fiancée, Jane Parker took part as one of the virtues. Anne Boleyn herself, appropriately enough as it would be shown, played the role of Perseverance.

Anne must have been thrilled at the prominence that she was given in the masque. The castle was defended by another eight ladies playing vices. They were dressed like women of the Indies and, whilst they defended the castle, eight lords entered dressed in cloth of gold and blue satin. They stormed the castle, which the ladies defended with rose water and comfits until the eight bad ladies were driven away. The eight virtues then came down from the tower and danced with the lords. Anne's partner is nowhere recorded but it must have been one of Henry's favourites. Henry himself is most likely to have danced with his sister, Mary or, perhaps, Mary Boleyn.

Mary Boleyn had been back at the English court for several years before Anne's arrival and Anne is likely to have heard something of Mary's reputation whilst she remained in France. By the time of Anne's return to England, Mary Boleyn was well established as Henry VIII's mistress. This was a very different relationship to the casual affair Mary had had with Francis I in France and the affair between Mary and Henry lasted for several years. It is possible that Mary's marriage in early 1521 to William Carey, a gentleman in Henry's privy chamber, was intended to protect her honour should she fall pregnant by the king. It is almost certain that she was already Henry's mistress by this time.

Mary Boleyn well-deserved the epitaph of 'Kindness' which was given to her in the court masque and she was eager to please and generous. Thomas Boleyn's rise to greater prominence during the early 1520s is probably linked to the position that his eldest daughter held with Henry and it is probable that Mary was encouraged to begin, and to continue, her affair with the king. Even if Thomas Boleyn was unhappy with his daughter taking the role of royal mistress, he must have been pleased with the tangible benefits he received from the relationship. In 1520 he was appointed Controller of the Household and in April 1522 he was promoted to Treasurer of the Household, both coveted positions. The king's affair with Mary Boleyn, which was almost at an end by 1525, was also behind Thomas Boleyn's elevation to the peerage on 16 June 1525 when he was created Viscount Rochford. Mary herself received few benefits from the relationship and, when it came to an end in the mid 1520s, she was simply discarded by the king. Anne would have taken note of her sister's treatment and it was something that she remembered in her own relationship with Henry. Anne Boleyn was a very different woman to her sister and would never be content with sacrificing her honour and her prospects of a good marriage for a few years of

Top: 21. Hatfield House, Hertfordshire. The childhood home of Anne's daughter, Elizabeth and the place where, in 1558, she was informed that she had become queen. *Below:* Staircase at Hatfield House. Princess Elizabeth's earliest home was intended to be a fitting residence for the heir to the throne when she was away from court.

22. Decoration outside the Chapel Royal at Hampton Court showing the entwined initials of Anne's successor, Jane Seymour with Henry's. Anne may never have recognised just how formidable a rival she had in Jane.

23. Traitor's Gate, under which Anne passed on her way into the Tower.

24. Catherine Howard, Anne's cousin and successor as Henry's wife shown as the Queen of Sheba in a window at King's College Chapel, Cambridge. Catherine would follow her cousin to the block less than six years after Anne's death.

25. The Tower of London. The formidable fortress in which Anne was imprisoned and spent her last days.

26. The chapel of St Peter ad Vincula on Tower Green with the scaffold site where Anne died in the foreground.

27. Anne Boleyn. Anne was noted for her black hair and captivating dark eyes.

28. A later artist's impression of Anne Boleyn showing evidence of her fate below the portrait.

29. Anne's father, Thomas Boleyn. Thomas recognised his youngest daughter's promise and always expected her to make an advantageous marriage.

THOMAS · DVKE · OFF · NORFOLK · MARSHALL
ND · TRESVRER   OFF · INGLOND

HE · LXVI · YERE   OF · HIS · AGE

30. Anne's uncle, the Duke of Norfolk. Norfolk was ambitious for his family and saw two of his nieces become the wives of Henry VIII.

31. Margaret of Austria. Anne's first appointment was with the regent of the Netherlands and Anne flourished at Margaret's cultured court.

32. Mary Tudor, the French Queen. Anne left Margaret of Austria to serve Mary Tudor in France and was a witness to the French Queen's secret disgrace.

33. Francis I of France. The French king was notoriously licentious and counted Anne's sister amongst his mistresses.

prominence at court, a few presents, a few honours for her father and a ship named after her in the royal fleet.

Unlike her sister, Anne was determined to look for an advantageous marriage when she returned to the English court. It is probable that she would have been happy to remain in France and that she would, eventually, have arranged a French marriage for herself. In 1522 both Anne's father and Cardinal Wolsey, Henry VIII's chief minister, had other ideas. Anne, however reluctantly, had been summoned home from France for a marriage.

In 1515 Anne's great-grandfather, the Earl of Ormond, had died. Ormond left only two daughters, the elder, Anne, who married into the St Leger family and the younger, Margaret, who was the mother of Thomas Boleyn. The Ormond title and lands were not entailed on the male line and the Earl's English possessions quickly passed to his St Leger and Boleyn heirs. In Ireland, the Earl's title and estates were claimed by his cousin, Sir Piers Butler, who declared himself Earl of Ormond soon after the old earl died. Thomas Boleyn immediately claimed the earldom from the king, pointing out that Butler had no legal right to it. However, the king, anxious not to offend a powerful Irish family, asked Wolsey to find a solution to the problem which did not involve stripping Butler of his claimed earldom and the Irish Ormond lands. It was Anne's uncle, the Earl of Surrey, who suggested a solution to Wolsey and it was quickly agreed by the king and the cardinal that Thomas Boleyn's only unmarried daughter, Anne, would marry Butler's eldest son, James. This match was formally proposed by the Irish Council to Henry in September 1520 and Thomas Boleyn was instructed to send for his daughter.

Anne had no say in the marriage negotiations conducted on her behalf and this cannot have been easy for her. It is possible that Anne employed some delaying tactics whilst the marriage negotiations were conducted and, certainly, the gap of over a year between the marriage being mooted and Anne's return to England suggests that neither she, nor her father, were entirely happy with the solution offered to the Ormond problem. Eventually, Anne was forced to bow to pressure and while she threw herself into court life in early 1522 the spectre of the Butler marriage would have been constantly hanging over her.

James Butler had been raised at the English court and Anne would almost certainly have met him shortly after her arrival in England. No details survive of the meeting between Butler and Anne but there is no evidence that they ever formed an attachment to each other. It appears that Anne quickly set her mind against the marriage, perhaps not relishing the prospect of banishment to Ireland. While the marriage had the approval of the king, it was gradually allowed to drift away and, by May 1523, Piers Butler had come round to the view that the marriage would not happen and he would need to defend his claim by force. It is likely that Thomas Boleyn, who always appeared lukewarm at the prospect of the match, had made difficulties, hoping to achieve the earldom for himself rather than the descendants of his daughter. Equally, it may have been Anne's own behaviour that helped scupper the match and, as Anne's biographer George Wyatt pointed out, 'she was indeed a very wilful woman'.

Anne quickly decided that she would not marry James Butler. Although, for Anne, the Butler marriage was dead, negotiations dragged on for some time and she would have known that no other marriage would be arranged for her whilst this marriage retained the support of the king. Anne, as a sixteenth century woman, was very aware that her future prospects lay in making a good marriage and she immediately set about arranging such a marriage for herself. This was an entirely unusual step for a woman to take and one which, once again, shows Anne's defiance of convention and her independent spirit.

Anne also had a high opinion of her worth and her choice of a husband fell on Henry Percy, heir to the earldom of Northumberland. Percy was a member of Wolsey's household in 1522 and Anne would have seen him regularly, noting his attachment to her. The relationship moved fast, probably at Anne's instigation and, according to William Cavendish, in his *Life of Wolsey:*

'My lord Percy, the son and heir of the Earl of Northumberland, then attended upon the Lord Cardinal, and was also his servitor. And when the lord Cardinal chanced at any time to go to the court the Lord Percy would then resort for his pastime unto the queen's chamber, and there would fall in dalliance among the queen's maidens, being at the last move conversant with Mistress Anne Boleyn than with any other. So that there grew such a secret love between them that at length they were engaged together, intending to marry'.

Percy fell completely in love with Anne, even to the extent of defying his father and entering into a secret engagement with her. Anne's feelings for Percy are less clear. Certainly, a marriage with Henry Percy was a very grand match for her and one that would usually have been out of her reach. It is almost certain that the prospect of becoming Countess of Northumberland would have been the first consideration for the practical and ambitious Anne. However, it is possible that she also had feelings for Percy coincidental to the advantages of the match. Henry Percy was aged around twenty in 1522, a similar age to Anne and the couple may well have had interests in common. Anne's enmity towards Wolsey also stems from his interference in this match. It is possible that she bore him a grudge for the loss of her future position as Countess of Northumberland. This would seem unlikely since, by the time she acted against the Cardinal, Anne knew that she would become queen. It seems more likely that Anne's feelings were hurt by the Cardinal's interference and the loss of her relationship with Percy.

Anne was pleased with the effect that she had on Henry Percy and she willingly entered into an engagement with him as soon as he asked. The exact nature of the engagement between Anne and Percy has often been debated and the formalities that they did or did not go through in establishing the connection would have a dramatic effect on their future lives. In 1532 Percy's wife, Mary Talbot, whom he was forced to marry soon after the end of his relationship with Anne, claimed to the king that her husband had entered into a binding betrothal with Anne. The Percys' marriage was notoriously unhappy and this was probably a move by the Countess to attempt to secure her own divorce on the basis that Anne had been precontracted to Percy. This was also something that would be raised, to much greater effect, in the days leading up to Anne's death.

In the sixteenth century, a precontract was taken to be as binding as marriage and the existence of an earlier precontract was a legitimate ground for divorce. In 1483 Richard, Duke of Gloucester, was able to invalidate the marriage of his brother, Edward IV, on the basis that the king had earlier entered into a precontract. Given this security, precontracts were frequently consummated and Anne and Percy would both have considered themselves married following their engagement and it is likely that they also consummated their relationship.

Henry Percy, of all Anne's earlier suitors, is the man that Anne Boleyn is most likely to have consummated her relationship with. It was the Percy engagement which kept coming back to haunt Anne in her later life and Anne, who was not prepared to throw herself away without a secure promise of marriage, may well have been prepared to consummate her relationship in the hope of concluding the marriage more quickly. This was certainly Anne's tactic in her relationship with Henry VIII and, once she was certain that she would be married soon, Anne was happy to consummate her relationship to ensure that marriage was achieved more quickly.

There is also a tantalising hint that Anne was a woman with a past in her own correspondence. An unusual letter was written by Anne in 1532 before her marriage to Henry VIII. Anne wrote to a Lady Wingfield, who was probably a member of Henry's court. In this letter Anne took an unusually subservient tone:

> 'Madam, though at all times I have not shewed the love that I bear you as much as it were indeed, yet now I trust that you shall well prove that I loved you a great deal more than I made fayn for, and assuredly, next to mine own mother, I know no woman alive that I love better'.

Anne's letter continues in the same tone and it is clear that she was anxious to remain on friendly terms with Lady Wingfield. The reason for Anne's desperate need to keep Lady Wingfield friendly is not clear but it also appears that a deathbed confession by Lady Wingfield, of something that she knew about the queen, was used in the investigation into Anne that ultimately led to her arrest and execution. Lady Wingfield was, perhaps, present at court during Anne's relationship with Henry Percy. She may have been friendly with Anne and learned the secret that Anne, considering her marriage to Percy to be a certainty, agreed to consummate the relationship. When Anne later became involved with the king this was a secret that she would have wanted to keep at all costs and there is no doubt that Anne's relationship with Percy was used by the king when he wanted to be rid of her. As the example of one of Anne's successors as Henry's wife, Catherine Howard, shows, a lack of premarital chastity was a potential reason for removal from court, something that Anne would have wanted to avoid at all costs.

A question mark must certainly hang over whether or not the relationship between Anne and Percy was consummated, but it is possible. Be that as it may, however, the relationship itself was doomed. Anne probably hoped to be securely married to Percy before word of the attachment became commonly known. This was not to be and it 'came to the king's knowledge. Who was much offended'. It seems likely that the king, who in 1522 or 1523 had no interest in Anne, was angered by the match given the disparity between the potential bride and groom. He instructed Wolsey to break the engagement and Wolsey summoned Percy to him, rebuking him and ordering him to break off his attachment to Anne as she was beneath him in rank.

Faced by the wrath of the Cardinal, Henry Percy burst into tears. He did attempt to defend Anne, demonstrating his love for her. Percy, in spite of his terror, answered the Cardinal that:

> 'I considered that I was of good years, and thought myself sufficient to provide myself with a convenient wife whereas my fancy served me best, not doubting but that my lord my father would have been right well persuaded. And though she be a simple maid, and has but a knight to her father, yet is she descended of right noble parentage. For by her mother she is near to the Norfolk blood: and on her father's side lineally descended from the Earl of Ormond, he being one of the earl's heirs general'.

Anne must have coached Percy in her family history. However, in spite of what Percy claimed, he knew full well that his father could never be persuaded to agree to the match. Wolsey was angered by Percy's defiance and sent for his father. Percy might have had the courage to try to stand up to Wolsey but he was no match for his own father and the old Earl of Northumberland commanded Percy to break the engagement and whisked him away from court, marrying him quickly to Lady Mary Talbot.

Percy's marriage to Mary Talbot was a much more suitable match for him as she was one of the daughters of the Earl of Shrewsbury but the marriage was notoriously unhappy and the couple separated after their only child was stillborn. Once Anne began her relationship with the king it also became very dangerous to stand as a possible impediment to her marriage and Percy would always strongly deny that there had been any precontract between them. In a letter written at the time of Anne's fall, Percy, perhaps concerned that he might fall with her, wrote angrily to Thomas Cromwell refuting any suggestion of an engagement between him and Anne:

> 'This shall be to signifie unto you that I perceive by Sir Raynold Carnaby, that there is supposed a precontract between the queen and me; whereupon I was not only heretofore examined upon my oath before the Archbishopps of Canterbury and York, but also received the blessed sacrament upon the same before the Duke of Norfolk, and other the king's highnes' council learned in the spiritual law;

assuring you Mr Secretary by the said oath, and blessed body which affore I received, and hereafter intend to receive that the same may be to my damnation, if ever there were any contracte or promise of marriage between her and me'.

This letter was written on the day before Anne's death and was an attempt by Percy to ensure that he was in no way implicated in her fall. At the time of his relationship with Anne he probably viewed matters between them very differently.

Percy may also, perhaps, have pined away without Anne and he spent the rest of his life suffering from ill health and invalidism. Percy was beset by some ailment throughout his adult life and in 1529 it was reported that his old disease had returned and that his death was expected. He was also ill in 1532, 1533 and 1534 and in February 1536 he reported that he had not left his chamber for more than a year. Percy outlived Anne, but only by a year, and died in his mid thirties. It is unclear what the nature of his illness was but it is possible that it was psychological.

While Percy pined for Anne, Anne herself must have been furious. According to Wolsey's biographer, Cavendish, 'Mistress Anne Boleyn was greatly offended with this, saying that if it lay ever in her power she would work the Cardinal as much displeasure as he had done her'. This is the origin of Anne's enmity towards Cardinal Wolsey and she blamed him wholly for the loss of Henry Percy. She was however, not in a position to act against the Cardinal in 1522 or 1523 and she was sent away from court in disgrace. Anne's relationship with Percy is the first indication of her independent mind and her ability to subvert the norms of society. It is also the first indication of just how attractive she was to men and she quickly had another admirer.

CHAPTER 5

Fair Brunet

Anne must have felt humiliated and angry on her arrival at Hever following the end of her engagement to Henry Percy. She spent her time idly waiting for a summons back to court and the signal that she had been forgiven. For Anne, who was used to the glamour of the French court and the fast-pace of the English court, Hever must have seemed a tedious backwater. Her rustication to Hever did however allow her to reacquaint herself with a Kentish neighbour, Thomas Wyatt, and Anne was quick to embark on her next flirtation. Whatever Anne's feelings for Henry Percy, she would have known that, following his marriage, he was lost to her forever.

Thomas Wyatt is the second man with whom Anne was romantically linked. He came from an old Kentish family associated with the Boleyns. His father, Sir Henry Wyatt, was a neighbour of Thomas Boleyn and they were both created knights of the Bath at Henry VIII's coronation. They also shared the office of constable of Norwich castle from 1511, something which must have brought them and their respective families into contact with each other. Thomas Boleyn was also probably Thomas Wyatt's godfather. No record of Anne and Wyatt's early relationship exists but it is inconceivable that they would not have come into contact during Anne's years of exile at Hever. The two families would have socialised regularly with each other when they were in the country and Anne may well have been attracted to Wyatt as a source of information about the court from which she was banished.

By 1525 Thomas Wyatt was a rising star at court and was held in high esteem by everyone there. He was a true renaissance figure: handsome, athletic and a poet. He was of a similar age to Anne and she is likely to have been flattered by his attentions. Wyatt also found himself fascinated by the exotic Anne and as well as being attracted to her appearance he was also intrigued by her 'witty and graceful speech, his ear also had him chained unto her, so as finally his heart seemed to say, I would gladly yield to be tied for ever with the knot of love'. Wyatt may have offered his heart to Anne forever but both she and he would have been well aware that he could offer Anne nothing so permanent. In spite of his profession of undying love for Anne, Wyatt was already married.

Anne knew full well that Wyatt was married and, according to her biographer, Wyatt's own grandson, she rejected him outright because of this. She did this gently, still enjoying a flirtation with him and knowing that Wyatt's attentions 'might the rather occasion others to turn their looks to that which a man of his worth was brought to gaze at in her'. Anne was, after all, still looking for a husband and Wyatt's interest would have served to increase the interest of other more eligible men. She may also still have been grieving for her forced separation from Henry Percy and a flirtation with Wyatt would have taken her mind off her loss. Wyatt's visits to Kent also provided a useful distraction to Anne from her life in the country. The wait must have seemed endless but, at last, the summons to court came and by late 1525 or early 1526 Anne Boleyn was back in the household of Queen Catherine. She did not forget her friendship with Wyatt however and their flirtation continued upon her return to court.

There is no doubt that Anne and Wyatt quickly began some kind of relationship and that Wyatt cherished hopes that it would be consummated. The exact nature of the relationship has often been debated. Certainly, Wyatt was in love with Anne and several of his poems plainly refer to her and speak of his love for her. To Wyatt, Anne was the exotic 'Brunet' and it is clear that it was her dark looks that drew him to her, as it did with her other suitors. One poem of Wyatt's written some time after his affair with Anne speaks of her place in his heart:

'Be sign of love. Then do I love again,
If thou ask whom, sure since I did refrain
Brunet that set my wealth in such a roar
The unfeigned cheer of Phyllis hath the place
That Brunet had: she hath and ever shall'.

That Wyatt wrote this poem to refer to Anne is clear from his original draft. The third line quoted above originally read

'Her that did set our country in a rore'. Anne was mysterious and glamorous and Wyatt was in love with her, as his own poems demonstrate.

Wyatt had been married for several years before he became interested in Anne but it would appear that the marriage was always unhappy. Anne may have awakened in Wyatt feelings that he did not have for his wife. Wyatt's marriage proved to be disastrous and, by some point before 1526, he had denounced his wife for adultery, refusing to maintain her. This separation proved to be permanent and, by 1541, Wyatt was openly living with Elizabeth Darvell, a maid of Queen Catherine Howard. Although Wyatt's separation from his wife coincides with his relationship with Anne it is unlikely that she was the cause of the breakdown and she would have been very much aware that Wyatt would be unlikely to secure a divorce. Wyatt's marriage had always been tumultuous and his love for Anne is likely to have been kept entirely separate from his domestic woes.

While Wyatt was in love with Anne, her feelings for him are less clear. One sixteenth century writer went so far as to suggest that Anne was 'passionately in love' with him. A number of accounts also suggest that the relationship between Anne and Wyatt might have been less platonic than that suggested by George Wyatt.

This is certainly the view of the anonymous author of the *Chronicle of King Henry VIII*, which is contemporary with Anne. The anonymous Spanish chronicler claimed that, before Henry VIII married Anne, Wyatt came to him and said that he should not marry her as 'she was a bad woman'. According to the *Chronicle*, Henry refused to listen to Wyatt, sending him away furiously but Wyatt managed to get a letter to Henry at the time of Anne's death. Wyatt apparently wrote:

'Your Majesty knows that before marrying Queen Anne you said to me, Wyatt, I am going to marry Anne Boleyn, what do you think of it? I told your Majesty then that you had better not do so, and you asked me why; to which I replied that she was a bad woman, and your Majesty ordered me to quit your presence for two years'.

In this letter Wyatt continued saying that, driven by lust for Anne, he had arrived one night at her home and climbed into her room. Wyatt found Anne in bed and, on seeing him she exclaimed 'Good God! Master Wyatt, what are you doing here at this hour?'. Wyatt replied 'Lady, a heart tormented as mine has been by yours for long past has urged me hither to ask for some consolation from one who has caused it so much pain'. Anne then allowed Wyatt to kiss her and to move to even greater familiarities before a great stamping in the room above disturbed them and Anne rushed upstairs. When she returned over an hour later, Anne sent Wyatt away peremptorily and, according to the story, Wyatt later suspected that she must have had another lover upstairs.

The Chronicle of Henry VIII is contemporary with Anne and suggests not only that Anne was prepared to consummate her relationship with Wyatt but that she also took other lovers. This story clearly formed the basis of two later accounts written during the reign of Anne's daughter, Elizabeth, and intended to be unfavourable to the queen and her mother. One writer, Nicholas Harpsfield, wrote that Wyatt also informed the king that Anne was not a fit wife for him and that he had had 'carnal pleasure with her'. The Catholic propagandist, Sander, claimed that Wyatt had informed the council of 'how shameless Anne's life had been'. In his account, the Council agreed that 'Anne Boleyn was stained in her reputation' and no fit wife for the king. According to Sander, the Council rushed to inform Henry of Wyatt's disclosure:

> 'Henry was silent for awhile, and then spoke. He had no doubt, he said, that the council, in saying these things, was influenced by its respect and affection for his person, but he certainly believed that these stories were the inventions of wicked men, and that he could affirm upon oath that Anne Boleyn was a woman of the purest life'.

Sander claims that Wyatt was angry with the king's response and offered to arrange a meeting with Anne so that the king could see for himself. Henry angrily refused saying that Wyatt 'was a bold villain, not to be trusted'. Both Sander and Harpsfield claim that Wyatt and Anne had a sexual relationship. Sander even went further to claim that Wyatt was only one of many lovers for Anne and that her first had been her father's butler when she was only fifteen.

It is impossible now to say for certain whether Anne and Wyatt consummated their relationship. The account of the *Chronicle of Henry VIII* and later writers have often been believed and it has been claimed that Anne had several lovers before her marriage to the king and acquired a reputation for not being chaste. It is certainly true that Wyatt was arrested at the time of Anne's fall along with several other young men accused of adultery with Anne, and Wyatt was one of only two that survived. It is therefore possible that the *Chronicle's* claim is correct, that it was Wyatt's disclosure of his relationship with Anne before her marriage that saved him. However, the *Chronicle*, although contemporary, does not appear to have been written by someone who moved in royal circles and it is just as likely that Wyatt was saved by the king's affection for him than by claims that he had had sexual relations with Anne. It is also implausible that Wyatt would have remained in favour after disclosing that he had slept with the king's fiancée and, as George Wyatt pointed out, such a disclosure would almost certainly have broken the marriage. Anne was no fool and was determined to make the best marriage that she could. No evidence that survives of her character suggests that she would have risked ruining her prospects by sleeping with a married man. George Wyatt in his *Life of Queen Anne,* perhaps best sums up the unlikelihood of Anne agreeing to consummate her relationship with Wyatt 'for that princely lady, she living in court where were so many brave gallants at that time unmarried, she was not like to cast her eye upon one that had been then married ten years'. Wyatt, as a married man, was a very different proposition to Henry Percy and it is inconceivable that Anne, who stood out against the married king for so long, would have risked throwing herself away on Wyatt.

That Wyatt and Anne's relationship was also one of flirtation and pursuit on his part and aloofness on hers is clear from another of Wyatt's poems. This poem makes it clear that whilst Wyatt chased Anne she would never consent to be his and, as a married man, he was the least of her suitors:

'Whoso list to hunt: I know where is an hind
But as for me, alas I may no more;
The vain trevail hath wearied me so sore,
I am of them that farthest cometh behind.
Yet may I by no means my wearied mind
Draw from the deer, but as she fleeth afore
Fainting I follow, I leave off therefore,
Sithens in a net I seek to hold the wind.
Who list to hunt, I put him out of doubt,
As well as I may spend his time in vain,
And graven with diamonds in letters plain
There is written her fair neck round about:
'Noli me tangere, for Caesar's I am,
And wild for to hold, though I seem tame".

Anne allowed herself to be pursued and she enjoyed the chase, encouraging her pursuers where necessary. As Wyatt found, she was unavailable to anyone who could not offer her marriage and she certainly had other suitors. Anne Boleyn caused a sensation on her return to court and 'she drewe all mens thoughts and sett upon her the highest, and deerest price of woorthiness'. The names of these other suitors are no longer recorded and within a few months of her return to court Anne had another, much greater suitor, who had first noticed her due to her relationship with Wyatt.

Henry VIII's affair with Anne's sister, Mary, had ended some time before 1526. He was therefore looking for a new mistress during the early months of that year when he first noticed the object of his friend, Wyatt's, affections. Wyatt may not, at first, have realised how serious the king's feelings were and he attempted to compete with the king for Anne. One day, while Wyatt was in conversation with Anne, he playfully stole a small jewel from her which she kept hanging on a lace from her pocket. Anne immediately asked for it back but Wyatt refused, wearing it around his neck as a trophy and 'promising to himself either to have it with her favour or as an occasion to have talk with her'. Anne ignored Wyatt after her first appeals for the jewel were not successful and it was simply part of the affectionate way in which their flirtation was conducted. Anne probably enjoyed the attention, knowing that Wyatt, as a married man, was harmless and could cause her no difficulties with her other suitors.

Anne probably quickly forgot all about the jewel that Wyatt stole. Some time afterwards, while she was talking to the king, Henry also took a jewel from Anne, taking her ring to wear on his little finger. The king wore this trophy proudly, perhaps seeing it as the first sign that Anne returned his affection. He was still wearing the ring a few days later when he invited Wyatt and some other gentlemen to join him in a game of bowls. Flushed from his success with Anne, Henry was in an excellent mood and claimed to have won a game when it was clear that he was not the winner. The other team cautiously protested:

'And yet, still he pointing with his finger whereon he wore her ring, replied often it was his, and specially to the knight he said, Wiat, I tell thee it is mine, smiling upon him withal. Sir Thomas, at length, casting his eye upon the king's finger, perceived that the king meant the lady whose ring that was, which he well knew, and pausing a little, and finding the king bent on pleasure, after the words repeated again by the king, the knight replied, and if it may like your majesty to give me leave to measure it, I hope it will be mine; and withal took from his neck the lace whereat hung the tablet, and therewith stooped to measure the cast, which the king espying, knew, and had seen her wear, and therewithal spurned away the bowl, and said, it may be so, but then am I deceived; and so broke up the game'.

Henry was furious with Wyatt and stormed away to speak to Anne who, according to George Wyatt, managed to reassure the king of her innocence. This may have been the first moment that Henry came to realise how seriously he felt for Anne Boleyn.

Following the game of bowls, Wyatt was sent away for a time to ensure that the way was clear for the king to make his advances. Wyatt's appointment as Marshall of Calais in 1528 also suggests that the king wanted him out of the way and the poet was only permitted to return in 1532 when the king was, for the first time, sure that his marriage to Anne was a certainty. Wyatt was certainly not in disgrace and the appointment in Calais was a prestigious one. It is likely that Henry wanted to ensure that there was no rival for Anne's affections at his court. Anne retained an affection for Wyatt throughout her life and he played a prominent role at her coronation in 1533. He was also involved in her fall and was perhaps saved only by his enforced exile from Anne.

Anne Boleyn and Thomas Wyatt enjoyed a flirtation that could never lead to anything more due to the fact of Wyatt's marriage. By the middle of 1526 Anne found herself in a very similar relationship and one that would ultimately be much more significant for both her and England as a whole. Although Henry VIII would originally have considered Anne as a potential mistress, his relationship with her quickly turned to a deep obsession and the most serious love affair he was ever to have.

CHAPTER 6

For Caesar's I Am

In 1526 Henry VIII was thirty-five years old and in his prime. Handsome, cultured and athletic, the king was well known for his affairs with women of the court and, at the beginning of the year, he found himself without a mistress. Henry always drew his mistresses and English wives from the selection of women at his court and the incident of his game of bowls with Thomas Wyatt demonstrates that his eye quickly turned to Anne following her return to court.

Henry VIII would have at first considered only a flirtation with Anne when she came to his attention through Wyatt. Henry wanted a casual mistress and, after Anne's sister, Mary, had already filled that role, he may well have thought that Anne was the perfect candidate. It is unclear when Henry first began to look more seriously at his friend Wyatt's exotic mistress, but in February 1526 he arrived at a joust wearing the motto 'Declare I dare not'. This may be the first external sign of his love for Anne and the confusion he felt over his relationship with her. Henry also very clearly wanted to warn Wyatt away from Anne with his display of her ring during the game of bowls and he probably also ensured that her other suitors abandoned their suits. While it was Wyatt that first brought Anne to Henry's attention, the king quickly became fascinated with her and he was determined to ensure that he was her only suitor. The king rarely needed to warn anyone twice and, with Henry's interest declared, Wyatt and Anne's other suitors quietly abandoned their chase of her noting that, as Wyatt suggested, Anne was off limits and marked 'for Caesar's I am'.

In his early days as king, Henry had been described as the most handsome man in Europe and Anne, who clearly had an eye for a handsome man, cannot but have been flattered by Henry's attentions towards her. Snaring Henry Percy and Thomas Wyatt greatly increased Anne's sense of her own self-worth and this was further enhanced when she first noticed the king's attentions. Anne quickly joined in the flirtation with Henry but she also attempted to keep her distance. Anne was looking to arrange a grand marriage for herself and she may well have seen the king's favour as a way of attracting a high ranking and unmarried suitor. The strength of the king's feelings would have caught her by surprise.

By 1526, Henry had been married to Catherine of Aragon for nearly seventeen years. Although he had stopped sleeping with his wife by around 1524, Anne would have known that Henry was still very much married and unavailable for anything more than the kind of affair that her sister had enjoyed. Mary Boleyn had been Henry's mistress for several years but, by 1526, she had been discarded with little to show for her intimacy with the king. Anne knew from her own sister's example that the position of royal mistress was both fleeting and dangerous. Mary Boleyn had entirely lost her reputation and Anne, as the more ambitious sister, was not prepared to follow.

Although Anne is usually criticised for her overweening ambition it is very likely that thoughts of marriage did not, at first, enter her mind. As the niece of the Duke of Norfolk and the great-granddaughter of the Earl of Ormond, Anne had a high opinion of herself and she knew that her virtue was one of the best ways of securing a husband. Since Henry could not marry her she probably enjoyed a mild flirtation with him but, ultimately, stopped short of agreeing to become his mistress. Anne followed the example of Henry's own grandmother, Elizabeth Woodville, another Englishwoman who had attracted the interest of a king. According to Thomas More in his *History of Richard III*, Elizabeth also flirted with her king, Edward IV:

'Whose appetite, when she perceived, she virtuously denied him. But that did she so wisely and with so good manner, and words so well set, that she rather kindled his desire than quenched it; And finally after many a meeting, much wooing and many great promises, she well espied the king's affection towards her so greatly increased that she dared somewhat more boldly say her mind, as to him whose heart she perceived more finally set than fell off for a word. And in conclusion she showed him plain that as she wist herself too simple to be his wife, so thought herself too good to be his concubine'.

The difference between Elizabeth Woodville and Anne Boleyn was that Anne's king was certainly not offering her marriage in early 1526. Wearied by her attempts to keep the king at a distance, Anne retired home to Hever, perhaps hoping that he would find some other interest at court. Henry was unable to forget the aloof and mysterious Anne and he quickly inundated her with a series of letters. In these, Henry poured out his feelings towards Anne and, ultimately, made his decision concerning her and their future together. No one had ever said no to Henry before and it only served to fuel his passion and to ensure that his relationship with Anne was anything but short-lived. Anne was like no other woman Henry had ever met and with her dark, foreign looks, graceful manner and high-estimation of her own self-worth, she drove the king into a wild and uncontrollable lust for her.

Seventeen of Henry's letters to Anne survive, showing just how deeply in love with her he had become. These can be dated to 1526 and 1527 when Henry and Anne were often apart and chronicle the king's growing obsession with the exotic and elusive Anne Boleyn. Although Anne's own replies do not survive, it is possible to gain some idea of her response from Henry's letters. It is also clear that Henry was completely confused by the signals that Anne gave him and desperate for her to love him in return. All Henry's letters are in his own handwriting. This in itself shows something of the depth of his feeling for Anne as Henry hated writing and would dictate both private and public correspondence. For Henry, Anne was worth the discomfort of picking up a pen himself.

Anne was constantly on Henry's mind whether she was at court or away and in one letter he wrote stating that 'I and my heart put ourselves in your hands, begging you to recommend us to your good grace and not to let absence lessen your affection, for it were a great pity to increase that pain, seeing that absence does that sufficiently and more than I could ever have thought possible'. Henry was in an agony of self-doubt, terrified that Anne's absence from court would make her forget him. He continued:

'For although by absence we are parted it nevertheless keeps its fervency, at least in my case and hoping the like of yours; assuring you that for myself the pangs of absence is already too great, and when I think of the increase of what I must needs suffer it would be well nigh intolerable but for my firm hope in your unchangeable affection; and sometimes to put you to mind of this, and seeing that in person I cannot be with you, I send you now something most nearly pertaining thereto that is at present possible to send, that is to say, my picture set in a bracelet with the whole device which you already know; wishing myself in their place where it shall please you'.

Henry was simply not used to women refusing him and Anne Boleyn's aloofness made him obsessed with her. Anne, for her part, read Henry's letters eagerly. Safely away from him at Hever, she cannot but have been pleased at the effect she had on the king and she continued to send him mixed signals, both making it clear that she would not become his mistress, yet also trying to continue the flirtation.

Anne's approach confused Henry and he continued to send a stream of letters and messengers down to Hever in order to satisfy himself with news of Anne and to ensure that he was constantly on her mind. Anne was certainly constantly on his mind and in one letter he wrote of his dismay that Anne had decided not to return to court as planned, stating that 'it seems to me a very small return for the great love I have for you to be kept at a distance from the presence and person of the one woman in the world who I most esteem'. The frustration is plain from Henry's words and Anne must have been thrilled at the effect that she was having on the king, although she may also have relented a little to ensure that Henry remained as affectionate as ever. Henry finished his letter saying 'ponder well, my mistress, that absence from you is very grievous to me, hoping that it is not by your will that it is so; but if I understood that in truth you yourself wished it I could do no other than complain of my ill fortune while abating little by little my great folly'. There was a veiled threat in Henry's words that he expected Anne to be kind to him and Anne adapted her approach accordingly. It is likely that she still remained in great confusion however as to just what she was going to do with the love-struck king.

Whatever Anne's true feelings for Henry were in late 1526, Henry was certainly hopeful that she returned his love, writing anxiously to enquire about her health and to reassure Anne about his:

'My uneasy qualms regarding your health have much troubled and alarmed me, and I should have had no ease without certainty, but as you have not yet felt anything I hope and take for granted that it will pass you by as I trust it has with us; for when we were at Waltham, two ushers, two grooms of the chamber, and your brother, the Master Treasurer, fell ill and are receiving every care, and since then we have been well physicked in your house at Hunsdon, where we are well established and, God be praised, with no sickness, and I think that if you would leave the Surrey side as we did, you would pass without danger; and it may also comfort you to know it is true, as they say, that few women or none have this malady, and moreover none of our Court, and that few elsewhere have died of it. Wherefore I beg of you, my wholly beloved, to have no fear nor to be uneasy at our absence; for wherever I may be I am yours, although we must sometimes submit to fortune, for who wishes to struggle against fortune is usually very often the farther from his desire. Wherefore, comfort yourself and be brave, and avoid the evil as much as you can, and I hope shortly to make you sing for joy of your return. No more now for lack of time, except that I wish you between my arms that I might rid you somewhat of your unreasonable thoughts'.

Henry signed this letter 'written by the hand of him who is, and always will be, your Un H Rex changeable'. Henry was anxious to reassure Anne of his unchanged feelings for her and Anne may have been in need of some reassurance. The reference to Anne between Henry's arms suggests that she had already taken their relationship a step forward and she must have been uncertain about just where her relationship with Henry would lead.

An undated letter from Anne to Henry survives from this period and demonstrates that the confusion and uncertainty in the relationship was certainly not one-sided. Anne wrote:

'It belongs only to the august mind of a great king, to whom Nature has given a heart full of generosity towards the sex, to repay by favours so extraordinary an artless and short conversation with a girl. Inexhaustibly as is the treasure of your majesty's bounties, I pray you to consider that it cannot be sufficient to your generosity; for if you recompense so slight a conversation by gifts so great, what will you be able to do for those who are ready to consecrate their entire obedience to your desires? How great soever may be the bounties I have received, the joy that I feel in being loved by a king whom I adore, and to whom I would with pleasure make a sacrifice of my heart, if fortune had rendered it worthy of being offered to him, will ever be infinitely greater.

The warrant of maid of honour to the queen induces me to think that your majesty has some regard for me, since it gives me the means of seeing you oftener. And of assuring you by my own lips (which I shall do on the first opportunity) that I am,

Your majesty's very obliged and very obedient servant. Without any reserve, Anne Boleyn'.

Anne's letter shows that she responded to the king's affections and implies that she was also falling in love with him. Anne was still unsure as to just what he was offering her and had already made it clear that she would never accept the role that her sister had filled.

If Anne was in confusion about the future of her relationship with Henry, this was nothing compared to the confusion of the king who was utterly perplexed by the mixed signals she gave him. He searched desperately for some role that would please Anne and lead her to consent to becoming his mistress. Matters came to a head in early 1527 when Henry wrote to spill out all his doubts about Anne's feelings for him:

> 'In debating with myself the contents of your letters I have been put to a great agony; not knowing how to understand them, whether to my disadvantage as shown in some places, or to my advantage in others. I beseech you now with all my heart definitely to let me know your whole mind as to the love between us; for necessity compels me to plague you for a reply, having been for more than a year now struck by the dart of love, and being uncertain either of failure or of finding a place in your heart and affection'.

Anne must have been surprised at the effect that she had on Henry and that he had continued to pursue her for over a year. After a year of pursuit, Henry was also still desperate to make Anne his mistress and in the same letter he had a suggestion for her:

> 'If it pleases you to give yourself body and heart to me, who have been, and will be, your very loyal servant (if your rigour does not forbid me), I promise you that not only the name will be done to you, but also to take you as my sole mistress, casting off all others than yourself out of mind and affection, and to serve you only'.

Anne would have been shocked by the content of Henry's letter and he was making her a very different offer to the one that he had made previously. Henry, unable to live without Anne, made her the unprecedented offer of giving her the permanent role of royal mistress. This was still not marriage and still not what Anne required but it must have shown her just how serious the king's love for her had become. She probably replied indignantly, stating that whilst she loved him she was too good to be his mistress. Anne's refusal of the role of permanent royal mistress meant that there was only one option left for Henry if he wanted to have her. Both Anne and Henry knew that this was marriage.

Henry did not put his proposal to Anne in writing and he may have either sent a messenger to Anne at Hever or waited for one of her visits to court. It must still have been a shock to Anne however when the king finally offered to make her his wife and she insisted on time to consider his proposal. George Wyatt suggests that Anne was reluctant to agree to marry Henry as she loved Queen Catherine. It is more likely that she wanted time to discuss the matter with her father and to consider the seriousness of the king's offer. Thomas Boleyn 'was not a little joyful' when he heard of the proposal and this must have helped persuade Anne to accept the king. Anne was probably also attracted to Henry both as a man and as a king and she would have wanted to accept him, although she was also aware of the dangers of doing so.

Anne's feelings were in turmoil following the king's offer of marriage and she expressed this fact in a gift she sent to Henry along with her acceptance, both of which were very well received. Henry wrote:

'I thank you very cordially, not only for the handsome diamond and the ship in which the lonely damsel is tossed about, but chiefly for the fine interpretation and the humble submission which your kindness has made of it; thinking well that it could be very difficult for me to find occasion to merit it if I were not aided by your great indulgency and favour, for which I have sought, seek, and will ever seek, by everything in my power'.

It was clear to Henry that the storm-tossed damsel was Anne herself, beset by the troubles she would face in accepting him. He continued saying:

'The demonstrations of your affections are such, the beautiful words of the letter so cordially couched, as to oblige me ever truly to love, honour and serve you, begging you to continue in the same firm and constant purpose, assuring you that so far from merely returning your devotion I will out-do you in loyalty of heart were that possible, and you, with no bitterness in yours, can further that end; praying also that if at any time I have offended you, you will give me the same absolution as you yourself demand; again assuring you that henceforward my heart shall be dedicated to you alone, with a strong desire that my body could also be thus dedicated, which God can do if he pleases'.

Henry, ecstatic with happiness at Anne's promise, does not appear to have realised the difficulties that they would face before they could be married and signed his letter 'H seeks AB no other' with Anne's initials enclosed in the drawing of a heart. For the first time in his life, Henry was deeply in love and it is difficult to see how Anne cannot have returned some of this fervour. She would have been excited at the prospect of becoming a queen, a role she could never even have considered possible only a few short months before.

Anne did not set out to attract the king but she may also have been attracted to him in turn and this attraction would have turned to love as his devotion to her became evident. Henry was still one of the most handsome men in Europe and there can be no doubt that Anne was interested in him. Henry's marriage proposal was beyond Anne's wildest dreams and she hoped to marry quickly. This was also Henry's dearest wish and the prospect of marriage increased his lust for Anne. In one letter, when they were again separated, Henry begged Anne to return quickly to court, stating that he was 'hoping very soon to tell you by word of mouth the further pains I have suffered by your absence'. For a man who would eventually have six wives and several mistresses, Henry never knew passion like that which he felt for Anne Boleyn and, almost from the moment that she first came to his attention, she was his truest love and his obsession.

Anne Boleyn was well aware of Henry's love for her and worked hard to ensure that she maintained his interest. Although she always stopped short of consummating the relationship she and Henry also developed some degree of physical relationship over time and this may have been on the occasion of their promise to marry. In one letter Henry ended with 'wishing myself (especially of an evening) in my sweetheart's arms, whose pretty duckies [breasts] I trust shortly to kiss'. Anne was not entirely chaste in response to the king's ardent pursuit and it may have been all she could do to fend him off when she was with him. When Anne finally consented to be intimate with Henry she can never have imagined that it would be over five years before her marriage and the full consummation of their relationship would occur.

Anne must have foreseen that there would be difficulties ahead although she cannot have known just how long the journey to marriage would be. On 5 May 1527, Henry gave a banquet in honour of the French ambassadors and publicly led Anne out as his partner for the first time. Twelve days later a secret ecclesiastical court opened in London to try the validity of the king's marriage and, as Anne and Henry hoped, to clear the way for them to marry. In the spring of 1527 Anne believed that her marriage was imminent, providing that Henry could quickly obtain his divorce from Catherine of Aragon.

CHAPTER 7

The King's Great Matter

Anne and Henry believed in 1527 that it would be a relatively simple matter to secure his divorce. Henry's wife, Catherine of Aragon, had turned forty in 1525 and it was clear to everyone that she would bear Henry no further children. Henry and Catherine had only one surviving child, a daughter, Mary, and Henry believed that the entire world would agree that it was reasonable for him to make a new marriage to a younger and more fertile woman. He also knew that he had very good pretext for a divorce as Catherine was the widow of Henry's elder brother, Arthur.

Catherine of Aragon had married Arthur, Prince of Wales on 14 November 1501 at St Paul's Cathedral. The marriage had been a major ceremonial event of the reign of Henry VII, Henry VIII's father, and following their marriage, Catherine and Arthur travelled to Ludlow to rule his principality. The marriage was destined to be short lived however and Arthur died at Easter 1502, leaving Catherine a young widow and the young Henry VIII as prince of Wales. Neither Henry VII nor Catherine's parents, Ferdinand of Aragon and Isabella of Castile, wanted to lose their alliance and the young Henry was quickly betrothed to his brother's widow. The Bible was known to be contradictory on the subject of marriage with a deceased brother's wife and, to ensure that the marriage was not invalid, a dispensation was obtained from Pope Julius II allowing the couple to marry when Henry came to the throne in 1509.

Henry had been happy to marry Catherine in 1509 but, when he finally made the decision to marry Anne, he decided to use the possible doubts over his marriage to secure his divorce. In the Bible, Leviticus expressly states that a brother shall not marry his dead brother's wife and, if he does, the couple shall remain childless. Henry and Catherine's eldest son had died within a few weeks of his birth and, following this birth, Catherine experienced a sequence of miscarriages and stillbirths. The only exception was the birth in 1516 of Princess Mary but, as a girl, Mary was not enough for Henry. When he came to examine his marriage to Catherine he considered his lack of sons to be tantamount to childlessness. So he was confident that his marriage would quickly be shown to be against God's law and thus invalid. The Bible was in fact less clear cut than Henry was prepared to consider and the Book of Deuteronomy contains an express command for a man to marry his brother's wife should his brother die childless. Both Anne and Henry would have hoped that Leviticus would be considered the more applicable in Henry's case.

On 18 May 1527, soon after Anne had agreed to marry the king, Cardinal Wolsey summoned a church council at Westminster to consider the validity of Henry's marriage. Both Henry and Anne hoped that Wolsey would quickly pronounce the sentence of divorce and that they would be married within a matter of months. It was intended that the trial should be kept a secret in an attempt to prevent Catherine from appealing to her powerful nephew, the Emperor Charles V, before sentence could be given. Anne, kept in the background and unable to attend, waited anxiously as the hearing progressed. If Henry thought that he could keep the court secret however, he was very much mistaken and both Catherine and the Imperial ambassador knew of the proceedings within hours. Catherine asked the emperor to alert the pope so that he could stop Wolsey from pronouncing sentence and, on 31 May, Wolsey was forced to adjourn the court when it became clear just how widely known proceedings had become. This was the first setback for Anne and Henry and, although Anne would not have realised it, it was only the beginning of a very long wait to become queen.

Anne had been raised to see the king as an all-powerful figure and she expected that Henry could quickly secure his divorce, regardless of any opposition from Catherine's family. When the court was adjourned on 31 May and it became clear that Henry would have to seek his divorce from the Pope, both he and Anne may well still not have anticipated great difficulties in bringing about their marriage. All this changed however when news reached England that the emperor had sacked Rome on 16 June 1527 and was holding the Pope as a virtual prisoner. Both Anne and Henry knew that, with the

Pope in the hands of Catherine's nephew, the divorce was likely to become a much more lengthy process.

Anne was still a member of Catherine's household when news of the divorce leaked out and she must have found it difficult to remain silent as rumours flew around the court. Henry himself always claimed that his conscience was first pricked regarding his marriage due to a comment made by the Bishop of Tarbes, who was the French ambassador to England when a marriage was being arranged between Princess Mary and the Duke of Orleans. The Bishop suddenly broke off negotiations 'because (as he said) he was not fully persuaded of the legitimacion of the Ladie Marie beinge the king's daughter begotten of his brother's wife'. Henry always claimed that it was this that first alerted him to the invalidity of his marriage and that his desire for a divorce was based solely on his troubled conscience.

While this was the official reason, it was not widely believed either in England or in Europe. For Henry and Anne, however, it was a convenient claim to divert attention from their own relationship and Anne must also have been glad to hear rumours circulating at court which claimed that it was Wolsey who had set the king on the path to divorce. This was a widely held view and Catherine of Aragon herself believed that it was Wolsey who first suggested divorce to the king. It was also convenient for Anne, whose position was still not widely known, to allow the king's chief minister, and her greatest enemy, to bear the blame for the king's actions.

Anne found herself in a difficult position as word of the king's actions leaked out in the spring and summer of 1527. At this early stage, she feigned ignorance of the divorce and she must have been glad to be out of the queen's company as much as possible. Anne knew that, for all her apparent submissiveness and obedience, Catherine was a formidable opponent, and she cannot have failed to be aware of the popularity that Henry's wife enjoyed in England. Catherine of Aragon was viewed by many as almost a living saint. For example, the *Life of Jane Dormer*, which was written at the behest of a lady to Catherine's daughter, Mary, states that Catherine would pray on her knees without cushions and 'she was affable in conversation, courteous to all, and of an excellent and pious disposition'. The writer concluded that Catherine was a 'mirror of goodness'. While this is a highly partisan account, this is how Catherine was widely perceived. Anne must have felt increasingly uncomfortable as Catherine and her supporters began to watch her warily.

Anne and Catherine quickly became rivals. Catherine was less vocal in her enmity towards Anne, but she was able to find subtle ways to anger her opponent, just as Anne attacked her. According to George Wyatt, for example, Catherine would often insist on Anne joining her as she played cards so that Anne would be forced to display her small extra finger to the king. This must have greatly irked Anne and the card games would have been uncomfortable for both women. During one game Catherine finally confirmed that she knew full well what Anne's ambitions were:

> 'And in this entertainment of time they had a certain game that I cannot name then frequented, wherein dealing, the king and queen meeting they stopped, and the young lady's hap was much to stop at a king; which the queen noting, said to her playfellow, My lady Anne, you have good hap to stop at a king, but you are not like the others, you will have all or none'.

Anne was not close to Catherine and she is unlikely to have felt any remorse for her actions, instead allowing her ambition to drive her onwards. She must have found the proximity to her rival oppressive and she often spent time at Hever in the early years of the divorce proceedings.

When news of the imprisonment of the pope reached England, Henry immediately dispatched Wolsey to France to arrange an alliance. The Cardinal was still unaware that the king planned to marry Anne and it would have pleased Anne to know that her enemy could be of benefit to her unwittingly. Wolsey had always prided himself on delivering exactly what the king wanted and he would have felt certain that he could obtain the divorce, in spite of the difficulties caused by the Pope's imprisonment. While he was in France in July 1527 he tried to persuade the other cardinals to meet him at Avignon and to invest him with the necessary powers to exercise the Pope's authority. The Italian cardinals refused to leave Italy and Wolsey was forced to consider new steps to take.

By late June both Henry and Anne were fully committed to the divorce and on 22 June Henry finally informed Catherine officially of his 'concerns' over their marriage. Catherine already knew of the proceedings but it must have been difficult hearing the words directly from Henry and she promptly burst into tears. If Henry thought that Catherine would be compliant however, he was mistaken. As soon as she had been officially informed, Catherine wrote to her nephew for aid. Although Charles V barely knew his aunt, Catherine's treatment was a direct attack on his family's honour and he was not prepared to allow Henry to divorce her, whatever scruples of conscience he claimed to have. While in England Catherine was effectively powerless, in Rome she had the upper hand and it was necessary for Henry to send an ambassador to Rome 'lest the Queen should prevent us, by the Emperor's means, in our great matter'.

Henry and Anne did not at first realise the strength of Charles V's support for his aunt and they would have discussed their hopes that the emperor's support could be bought. Henry sent the Bishop of Worcester and his chaplain, Dr Lee, to Charles to attempt to persuade him to support the king. Charles clearly set out his position to the ambassadors, stating:

> 'That hee was sorry to understand of the intended divorce, adjuring the king (for the rest) by the Sacrament of Marriage, not to dissolve it or, if he would needs proceed therein, that the hearing and determining of the business, yet, might be refer'd to Rome, or a Generall Councill, and not be decided in England. Adding further, that he would defend the Queen's just cause'.

The emperor's position infuriated Henry and Anne although his response cannot have been entirely unexpected. At the same time that Henry's ambassadors travelled to the emperor, further ambassadors travelled to Rome.

In late 1527 Henry dispatched his secretary, Dr Knight, to Rome with secret instructions to request the king's divorce and, also, to obtain a dispensation to allow him to marry a woman related to him in the first degree of affinity. This is the first clear indication that Henry had decided to marry Anne and the dispensation, which was necessary due to his relationship with Mary Boleyn, would allow the couple to marry quickly. The Pope granted an audience to Knight and provided him with the necessary dispensation. He did not however grant the divorce and Henry quickly sent Edward Foxe and Stephen Gardiner to Orvieto to press the Pope further.

Anne kept a keen interest in the progress of the various embassies in Rome and she followed Foxe and Gardiner's progress with interest. She expected the ambassadors to contact her directly and, in a letter she wrote to Gardiner on 4 April 1529 regarding a later mission to Italy, she thanked him for the letter he had sent directly to her. She also expressed the hope that Gardiner's 1529 mission would be more pleasant to her than his first 'for that was but a rejoysyng hope, whiche causing [the lie] of it dose put me to the more payn, and they that ar parta[kers] with me, as you do knowe, and therefore I do trust that this herd begynn[ing] shall make a better endyng'. Gardiner and Foxe's first visit to Italy was a difficult one and they found the Pope in a pitiful state, protesting his loyalty to Henry and begging the ambassadors to give him more time. Foxe and Gardiner continued to press him and Foxe was able to return to England in April 1528 with some good news for Henry and Anne.

Foxe sailed from Calais on 28 April 1528 and travelled straight to Greenwich. He arrived in the evening and Henry commanded him to go straight to Anne's chamber. Anne was anxious to hear the news and, excitedly made 'promises of large recompense' to Foxe. Henry then entered the chamber and Anne left him alone with the ambassador for a few minutes. Foxe told Henry that the Pope was willing to satisfy the king as far as he was able and that he might be prepared to confirm a sentence of divorce given by his delegates in England. While this was not an absolute promise, it was the only progress in the divorce for almost a year and Henry called Anne in happily and instructed Foxe to inform her. Anne was overjoyed and the couple kept Foxe with them for most of the evening. Pope Clement VII was a timid man and in desperate fear of the emperor. After further pressing from Gardiner, he finally agreed on 11 June 1528 to send a papal legate, Cardinal Campeggio, to hear the case in England.

Anne and Henry were jubilant when they heard that Campeggio was to come to England. Cardinal Campeggio was no stranger to England and, as the Bishop of Salisbury, he had always been Henry and Anne's choice for the role of papal legate. The couple would not have suspected that Campeggio had been given secret instructions by the pope to delay matters as much as possible and Campeggio's progress towards England was painfully slow. By the end of June 1528, Campeggio had still not set out for England and Henry and Anne waited impatiently for news.

The summer of 1528 was a time of frustration for Henry and Anne as they waited for news of the legate. They also had other things on their minds when Anne found herself fighting for her life during that summer. In June 1528 there was an outbreak of sweating sickness in London which quickly infected much of the city. The sweating sickness was a terrifying disease. According to Du Bellay, the French ambassador, the sweat 'is a most perilous disease. One has a little pain in the head and heart; suddenly a sweat begins; and a physician is useless, for whether you wrap yourself up much or little, in four hours, sometimes in two or three, you are despatched without languishing'. Henry, always terrified of disease, was in a state of high anxiety as the sweat began to ravage the city. Even his love for Anne was not enough for him to brave infection and, when Anne herself began to experience the signs of the sweat, Henry ordered her home to Hever while he fled twelve miles to be safe from infection. Anne would perhaps have been angered by Henry's lack of constancy towards her but she was soon too ill to think of anything except survival.

Although Henry had fled from Anne, he quickly wrote to her to reassure her that his love for her remained unchanged. Anne was probably too ill to understand the content of Henry's letter when it arrived but it would have given some comfort to her when she regained consciousness. Henry wrote:

> 'There came to me suddenly in the night the most grievous news that could arrive, and I must need lament it for three reasons: the first being to hear of the sickness of my mistress, whom I esteem more than all the world, and whose health I desire as my own, and would willingly bear the half of your illness to have you cured; the second, for fear of being yet again constrained by my enemy absence, who until now has given me every possible annoyance, and so far as I can judge is likely to do worse, though I pray God to rid me of a rebel so importunate, the third, because the physician in who I most trust is absent at a time when he could do me most pleasure; for I hoped through him, and his methods, to obtain one of my chief joys in this world, that is to say, that my mistress should be cured'.

Henry instead sent his second doctor to Hever, something which must have been pleasing to Anne given the king's terror that he would succumb to the disease. He also added, demonstrating that his feelings for Anne were entirely unchanged: 'I hope soon to see you again, which will remedy me more than all the precious stones of the world'. Anne and her father both suffered from the worst symptoms of the sweat at Hever, but both miraculously survived. While Anne would have been gratified, as she lay recovering, that Henry had been very merry at court when he was informed of the news of his love's survival, she may also have remained angry at Henry for the speed at which he sent her away from court when she became ill.

Once news of Anne's survival reached Henry he sent a letter to her desiring that she return to court. Anne, probably enjoying her recuperation and Henry's obvious discomfort at her absence, delayed her return to London in spite of Henry's increasingly desperate pleas. In one letter, Henry attempted to tempt Anne back by telling her that he had ordered Wolsey to arrange lodging for her at court. He also sought to reassure her of his diligence in attempting to obtain the divorce, writing 'as touching our other affairs I assure you that there can be no more done; nor more diligence used, nor all manner of dangers better both foreseen and provided for; so that I trust it shall be hereafter to both our comfort'. He also refused to write the details of progress that had been made, instead stating that he would tell Anne when she arrived at court, 'trusting it shall not be long so, for I have caused my lord your father to make his provisions with speed'. He signed his letter 'written with the hand of him which I would were yours'. Anne wished this too, but she was not prepared to abandon her displeasure towards Henry quite so easily.

Anne remained at Hever for much of the summer. Henry continued to write his love letters to her however and she finally began to relent towards him, pleased at the effect that she had had on the king. In one letter, Henry wrote:

'The approach of the time which I have so long awaited rejoices me so much that it seems already here. However, the complete fulfilment cannot be until the two persons meet, which meeting, for my part, is more desirable than any other earthly thing; for what joy in this world can be so great as to regain the company of her who is the most loved; knowing also that she herself wishes likewise, the thought of which gives me great pleasure'.

Henry told Anne that her absence had given him 'the greatest pain at heart' and he begged her to tell her father to hurry her back to court. Henry signed the letter 'written by the hand of the secretary, who wishes himself to be with you privately, and who is, and ever will be your loyal and most assured servant'. Anne must have been pleased with Henry's obvious devotion to her and she finally rejoined him at court for a doubtless happy reunion.

Anne was still not officially a part of Henry's divorce and it was agreed that she would be kept in the background when Cardinal Campeggio arrived. She therefore retired from court sometime before Campeggio's arrival in England in October 1528. Henry continued to update her with news of the legate's progress, for example writing to inform her when Campeggio reached Paris and adding that 'I would you were in my arms and I in yours, for I think it long since I kissed you'. He would also have sent a message to Anne when Campeggio finally arrived in London on 8 October 1528 and immediately retired to his bed with gout. This was a disappointment and Anne was back at court for Christmas. This time, Anne had her own apartment at court as she did 'not like to meet with the queen'. Both Henry and Anne continued to place their hopes in the legate but they would have known, from the poor state of Campeggio's health, that it was likely to be a long process.

Campeggio finally rose from his sickbed in early 1529 and he quickly set about trying to fulfil his secret orders from the Pope, both to 'perswade the Queen to a Divorce; and disswade the King from it, as having either way the end he propos'd: yet he fail'd in both'. Campeggio then tried to persuade Catherine to become a nun. This would have been an acceptable solution to both Anne and Henry and it would have allowed the king to remarry in the lifetime of his first wife. From Catherine's point of view, it would have also have meant that the legitimacy of Princess Mary was unchallenged, something that she earnestly desired, but Catherine was a pious woman and could not bring herself to feign a vocation that she did not have. She had also been married to Henry for nearly twenty years and she was certainly in love with him and desperate to cling to her husband at all costs. Campeggio found both husband and wife unshakeable in their respective beliefs and commented of Henry that he was so convinced his marriage was void that 'if an angel was to descend from heaven he would not be able to persuade him to the contrary'. It quickly became apparent to Campeggio that the matter would need to be tried.

While preparations were put in place for the trial, Wolsey continued to try to find arguments in favour of the divorce. Through his examination of the original papal bull of dispensation, he thought he had found a flaw in that the wording said that Catherine's first marriage had been 'perhaps' consummated. Both Henry and Anne pounced on this triumphantly and Henry's lawyers argued that if Arthur and Catherine had consummated their marriage then it could never be valid. Catherine always claimed that she had been a virgin at the time of her marriage but Henry was able to find plenty of witnesses to suggest the contrary. George Earl of Shrewsbury, for example, was happy to testify that he had been present when Arthur had been conducted to Catherine's bedchamber and that he had always supposed that the marriage was consummated. A further testimony by Sir Anthony Willoughby was especially damaging to Catherine and he stated that Arthur had spoken to him on the morning after his wedding, saying 'Willoughby, bring me a cup of ale, for I have been this night in the midst of Spain'. Arthur also later boasted that 'it is good pastime to have a wife'. Catherine always insisted that her first marriage had been unconsummated and, given her deep religious faith, it seems unlikely that she was lying. Catherine's attempts to fight the divorce must have infuriated Anne. Catherine further angered Anne when she produced a copy of a papal brief which was held in Spain and which overcame all the difficulties Wolsey had identified in the papal bull.

Henry and Anne were taken aback at Catherine's production of the papal brief and an immediate search was made of the English records but no English copy could be found. Henry quickly declared that it must be a forgery and he ordered Catherine's counsel to persuade her to send for the original from Spain. Henry briefed Catherine's lawyers to tell her that 'If we ourselves were judges in this matter, and should lawfully find that where ye might ye did not do your diligence for the attaining of the said original, surely we would proceed further in that matter as the law would require, tarrying nothing therefore as if never any such brief has been spoken of'. Catherine dutifully agreed to write to the emperor requesting the original but she was not fooled. As soon as the letter was dispatched to Charles, Catherine also sent her chaplain Thomas Abel with instructions to tell the emperor that he must under no circumstances give up the brief. Henry and Anne were furious, but there was nothing they could do and Anne once again retired from court when the legate's trial was finally convened at Blackfriars in June 1529.

Both Henry and Catherine were cited to appear before Campeggio and Wolsey on the first day of the trial at Blackfriars on 18 June 1529. To everyone's surprise, Catherine heeded the summons and sat in her chair on the opposite side of the hall to Henry. As the court was opened, Catherine stood up and walked over to the king, kneeling at his feet. Catherine knew that the Blackfriars court was in no way impartial and she immediately appealed to Rome for the case to be heard there. She also knew how to make her point and, as she kneeled before Henry, she made the speech of her life:

> "Sir', quoth she, 'I beseech you for all the love that hath been between us, and for the love of God, let me have justice and right, take of me some pity and compassion, for I am a poor woman and a stranger born out of your dominion. I have here no assured friends, and much less impartial counsel. I flee to you as to the head of justice within

this realm. Alas! Sir, wherin have I offended you, or what occasion of displeasure have I deserved against your will and pleasure – now that you intend (as I perceive) to put me from you? I take God and all the world to witness that I have been to you a true, humble and obedient wife, ever comfortable to your will and pleasure, and never said or did anything to the contrary therof, being always well pleased and contented with all things wherein you had any delight or dalliance, whether it were in little or much. I never grudged in word or countenance, or showed a visage or spark of discontent. I loved all those whom ye loved only for your sake whether I had cause or no, and whether they were my friends or my enemies. This twenty years or more I have been your true wife and by me ye have had divers children, although it hath pleased God to call them out of this world, which hath been no default of me'.

Catherine continued, insisting that Henry had found her a virgin at their marriage, as well he knew. She begged him to let her remain as his wife. Finally, as a mortified Henry sat watching, she stood and left the hall. As Catherine was ordered to return she said 'it makes no matter, for it is no impartial court for me, therefore I will not tarry'.

Catherine refused to return to court. Without the queen, Henry pushed Campeggio to give sentence, something that the Pope had instructed he could not give. Finally, when it became clear that the king wanted his judgment, Campeggio stood and said that he would give no judgment, revoking the case to Rome. Campeggio's announcement caused uproar in the court and Suffolk roared that 'Cardinalls never did good in England'. At that point, both Henry and Anne would have heartily agreed and, after two years of hoping, it was clear to them both that Cardinal Wolsey had failed in his promise to obtain the divorce.

CHAPTER 8

The Night Crow

Anne Boleyn's grudge against Cardinal Wolsey dated from his interference in her relationship with Henry Percy and it smouldered throughout the early years of her relationship with the king. Anne was prepared to work with Wolsey when she thought that he could help her achieve her marriage to the king, but she was never happy with the power of the Cardinal and she always intended to bring him down if she could. The debacle at Blackfriars finally provided Anne with this opportunity.

Although Anne was Wolsey's enemy, she was fully aware of the king's confidence in his first minister and the need to dissemble in her treatment of the Cardinal. Anne was nothing if not patient and she may even have seen a certain irony in the fact that Wolsey, who was considered to be the man best able to achieve the divorce, should help in bringing her to power. A number of letters from Anne to Wolsey survive showing that she was forced to suffer his presence. In one letter Anne wrote:

'My lord,
After my most humble recommendation, this shall be to give unto your Grace, as I am most bound, my humble thanks for the great pain and travail that your Grace doth take in studying by your wisdom and great diligence how to bring to pass honourably the greatest wealth that is possible to come to any creature living, and in especial remembering how wretched and unworthy I am in company to his Highness, and for you I do know myself never to have deserved by deserts, that you should take this great pain for me, yet daily of your goodness I do perceive by all my friends, and though that I had no knowledge by them, the daily proof of your deeds doth declare your words and writing towards me to be true'.

It must have grated on Anne to write these words to her greatest enemy and she would also have known that any pains taken by Wolsey were for the king rather than any favour he felt towards her. Anne was prepared to keep up the pretence while it still looked possible for Wolsey to obtain the divorce and she continued by assuring the Cardinal that 'next unto the king's Grace, of one thing I make you full promise, to be assured to have it, and that is my hearty love unfeinedly during my life'. Both Anne and Wolsey would have been well aware of the insincerity behind Anne's words but they both needed to keep up the pretence.

Anne also ensured that pressure was kept on Wolsey to keep working towards the divorce. In one letter, written whilst she was with Henry, Anne took the lead in writing to Wolsey before insisting that Henry add a postscript. In this letter, Anne again took a subservient tone which must have been difficult for her, writing that 'I do know of the great pains and trouble that you have taken for me, both day and night'. She also claimed that she could never recompense such trouble sufficiently save 'in loving you, next unto the king's Grace, above all creatures living'. Once the pleasantries were over, Anne then pressed Wolsey for news in a manner which made it clear that only good news was expected 'My lord, I do assure you, I do long to hear from you news of the legate; for I do hope, and they come from you, they shall be good; and I am sure you desire it as much as I, and more, and if it were possible, as I know it is not'.

While Wolsey is very unlikely to have desired Anne Boleyn's marriage to the king, Henry's postscript made it very clear just how far Anne's influence over the king extended. The king wrote:

'The writer of this letter would not cease, till she had caused me likewise to set to my hand, desiring you, though it be short, to take it in good part. I ensure you, there is neither of us, but that greatly desireth to see you, and much more joyous to hear that you have scaped this plague so well; trusting the fury thereof to be passed, specially with them that keepeth good diet, as I trust you do. The not hearing of the legate's arrival in France, causeth us somewhat to muse; notwithstanding, we trust by your diligence and vigilancy (with the assistance of Almighty God) shortly to be eased out of that trouble'.

For Wolsey, the fact that Anne was so often with the king whilst he was absent must have been ominous and he resolved to try to cultivate Anne's goodwill towards him. He may, perhaps, have believed that this was working and, in a later letter, Anne thanked him for a present that he had sent to her. She also wrote 'I trust my lord to recompense part of your great pains; for the which I must require you in the meantime to accept my good will in the stead of the power', ending 'written with the hand of her that is most bound to be. Your humble and obedient servant Anne Boleyn'. If Wolsey believed that Anne had forgiven him, he was very much mistaken. She was happy to work with him while it looked as though he would help her achieve what she most desired but, following the debacle at Blackfriars, it became painfully clear to Anne that Wolsey could no longer assist her in securing the divorce.

Anne always blamed Wolsey for the loss of her betrothal to Henry Percy, a man that she may have been in love with, and she must have been further irked by the Cardinal's failure to simply accept the fact of her growing dominance over the king. The loss of her betrothal was not the only issue over which Anne and Wolsey clashed and, time and again, they found themselves on different sides of an issue with only the king to bind them together.

One such conflict between Anne and Wolsey concerned the nunnery at Wilton. Although Anne escaped the sweating sickness relatively unscathed, her brother-in-law, William Carey, was not so lucky, dying during the same outbreak. Anne was not close to her sister but she promised Mary that she would do something for Carey's family, approaching the king about her 'sister's matter'. Anne suggested to Henry that he appoint Carey's sister Eleanor, who was a nun at Wilton, as abbess of the same house following the death of the former holder.

In her promotion of the candidacy of Eleanor Carey, Anne placed herself directly at odds with Cardinal Wolsey who petitioned for the election of the prioress, Isabel Jordan. By 1528 Anne felt sure enough of the king's affections to risk an open conflict with Wolsey and Henry at first favoured the election of Eleanor Carey, presumably to please Anne. Wolsey was not content to allow himself to be beaten by Anne and he carried out an investigation into the nuns at Wilton. This was reported to the king who wrote in shocked tones to Anne setting out the reasons why Eleanor Carey could not become Abbess after all:

'As touching the matter of Wylton my lord Cardinal hath had the nuns before him and examined them, Master Bell being present, which hath certified me that for a truth that she [Eleanor Carey] hath confessed herself (which we would have had abbess) to have had two children by two sundry priests and further since hath been kept by a servant of the Lord Broke that was, and that not long ago; wherefore I would not for all the gold in the world cloak your conscience nor mine to make her ruler of a house which is of so ungodly demeanour, nor I trust you would not that neither for brother nor sister I should so destain mine honour or conscience; and as touching the prioress or dame Ellenor's eldest sister though there is not any evident case proved against them, and that the prioress is so old that of many years she could not be as she was named, yet notwithstanding, to do you pleasure I have done that neither of them shall have it; but that some good and well disposed woman shall have it'.

The revelation that Eleanor Carey had given birth to two children by two different priests may not have come as a complete surprise to Anne and she certainly cannot have been happy with Henry's difficulties of conscience. She must have been annoyed that it was Wolsey who had been the ruin of Eleanor Carey's candidacy although Anne was appeased to some extent by the king's assurances that Wolsey's candidate would also be denied the position. Anne's annoyance would have quickly turned to fury when Wolsey disregarded the king's command.

By 1528, Wolsey had been in power for nearly twenty years and he may have failed to recognise that the young and inexperienced king he had originally known had disappeared. Convinced that the prioress was the best candidate, he overruled both Anne and the king's commands and appointed Isabel Jordan in return for her assurances that 'I will in the mean season, by the advice of your chancellor, order my sisters in such religious wise and our monastery according to the rule of our religion, without any such resort as hath been of late accustomed'. Wolsey, accustomed to having pre-eminence in church matters in England, must have thought that he could easily explain away the appointment to the king and he was shocked by Henry's reaction.

Henry was embarrassed and furious at the Cardinal's actions and wrote angrily to Wolsey saying:

'Methink it is not the right train of a trusty loving friend and servant, when the matter is put by the master's consent into his arbitre and judgment (specially in a matter wherein his master hath both royalty and interest) to elect and choose a person who was by him defended; and yet another thing which must displeaseth me more, that is, to

cloak your offence made by ignorance of my pleasure, saying that you
expressly know not my determinate mind in that behalf'.

Henry would not accept Wolsey's protestations of ignorance,
pointing out to him that he had expressly said that 'his pleasure
is that in no wise the Prioress have it, nor yet Dame Elinor's
eldest sister for many considerations'. Henry knew how angry
Anne would be to hear that the prioress had been elected and
he was also embarrassed by the fact that, to Anne, Wolsey
had made him look as though he was not master in his own
kingdom. The tenor of Henry's letter certainly frightened
Wolsey and he replied immediately apologising and explaining
his actions. This was sufficient for Henry and he wrote to
Wolsey again saying 'wherefore, my lord, seeing the humbleness
of your submission, and though the case were much more
heinous, I can be content for to remit it, being right glad,
that, according to mine intent, my monitions and warnings
have been benignly and lovingly accepted on your behalf'.
Wolsey must have been relieved to receive Henry's forgiveness
and he would have felt that he had entirely escaped from any
danger. However, for Anne, the continuing appointment of
Isabel Jordan as Abbess of Wilton was a constant reminder of
the Cardinal's power and of her enmity towards him. In the
Wilton affair, Wolsey consistently failed to appreciate Anne's
increasing political prominence and influence over the king,
something which would later prove to his cost.

George Wyatt included a further incident in his *Life of
Queen Anne* which shows something of the rivalry between
Anne and the Cardinal. He placed this incident in his *Life*
after Anne's marriage which, given the Cardinal's death in
1530, cannot have been the case. The details of the incident,
although inaccurate in places, are likely to be largely correct
and show clearly how Wolsey vied with Anne for the king's
favour. According to Wyatt, Anne Boleyn had acquired a copy
of Tyndale's *Obedience of a Christian Man,* a banned book
which she then read, marking out passages that she thought
would be of interest to the king. Anne then left the book by her
window where it was picked up by one of her ladies. Anne's
lady was reading the book when her suitor came in to speak
to her, taking the book from her to see what it was. At that
moment, Anne called her lady to her, leaving the suitor alone
with the book. After he waited for the lady for some time, he
left, taking the book with him as he believed it to be hers.

The suitor met a gentleman of Wolsey's household as he was
walking and this gentleman borrowed the book and showed

it to Wolsey. Wolsey, seeing what it was, immediately sent for the suitor and questioned him about how he had come by a banned book. Wolsey decided to tell the king what he had learned and:

'in which meantime the suitor delivered the lady what had fallen out, and she also to the queen [Anne], who, for her wisdom knowing more what might grow thereupon, without delay went and imparted the matter to the king and showed him the points that she had noted with her finger. And she was but newly come from the king, but the Cardinal came in with the book in his hands to make complaint of certain points in which he knew the king would not like of, and withal to take occasion with him against those that countenanced such books in general, and specially women, and as might be thought with mind to go farther against the queen more directly if he had perceived the king agreeable to his meaning'.

Henry, looking through the book and seeing the notes that Anne had written 'turned the more to hasten his [Wolsey's] ruin'.

Once again, Wolsey badly misjudged Anne's influence over the king and it is possible that he never fully understood the power that she wielded. According to a number of sources, an astrologer had once told Wolsey that he would be destroyed by a woman and he assumed that this must be Catherine of Aragon as she always 'showed but little love towards him'. Wolsey was correct in assuming that Catherine was his enemy and, in their view of the Cardinal if in nothing else, Anne and Catherine were entirely in agreement. Catherine also went out of her way to make things difficult for Wolsey, for example, immediately after the trial at Blackfriars, both Wolsey and Campeggio went to see Catherine at Bridewell, presumably in a last attempt to persuade her to submit to the divorce. Catherine was determined to cause as much embarrassment to the Cardinals as possible and, when Wolsey asked to speak to her in private, she refused saying that there was nothing that he could say to her that she would not want everyone present to hear. Wolsey then attempted to speak to Catherine in Latin before she stopped him and told him to speak in English. Wolsey was embarrassed and frustrated by Catherine's enmity towards him but if he thought that she had the power to bring him down then he was very much mistaken. The woman who was responsible for the fall of Wolsey was Anne Boleyn, not Catherine of Aragon.

By the time of the Blackfriars trial, Anne kept state like a queen at court and she had constant access to the king. With the failure of the court, Anne felt that she had no more use for the Cardinal and she blamed him for the court's failure due to his lack of commitment towards her marriage. She finally felt in a strong enough position to openly show her feelings towards him. Soon after the failure of the court at Blackfriars, Anne wrote to Wolsey setting out her full hatred towards him:

'My Lord,
Though you are a man of great understanding, you cannot avoid being censured by everybody for having drawn on yourself the hatred of a king who had raised you to the highest degree to which the greatest ambition of a man seeking his fortune can aspire. I cannot comprehend, and the king still less, how your reverent lordship, after having allured us by so many fine promises about divorce, can have repented of your purpose, and how you could have done what you have, in order to hinder the consummation of it. What, then, is your mode of proceeding? You quarrelled with the queen to favour me at the time when I was less advanced in the king's good graces, and after having therein given me the strongest marks of your affection, your lordship abandons my interests to embrace those of the queen. I acknowledge that I have put much confidence in your professions and promises, in which I find myself deceived. But, in future, I shall rely on nothing but the protection of Heaven and the love of my dear king, which alone will be able to set right again those plans which you have broken and spoiled, and to place me in that happy station which God wills, the king so much wishes, and which will be entirely to the advantage of the kingdom. The wrong you have done me has caused me much sorrow but I feel infinitely more in seeing myself betrayed by a man who pretended to enter into my interests only to discover the secrets of my heart. I acknowledge that, believing you sincere, I have been too precipitate in my confidence; it is this which has induced, and still induces me, to keep more moderation in avenging myself, not being able to forget that I have been
Your servant'.

For Anne, Wolsey was entirely to blame for the court's failure and she worked hard to ensure that this was also the king's belief.

By 1529, Anne was secure enough in Henry's affections to work openly against the Cardinal and shortly after the failure of the Blackfriars trial she berated the king at dinner for his kindness towards Wolsey. According to a member of Wolsey's household, William Cavendish, Anne turned on the king saying 'is it not a marvellous thing to consider what debt and danger

the Cardinal hath brought you in with all your subjects?'.
Henry, confused by this, asked 'How so, sweetheart?'. Anne
had carefully planned her attack on Wolsey, continuing that
'there is not a man within all your realm, worth five pounds,
but the Cardinal indebted you unto him by his means'. This
was a reference to a forced loan that Henry had received
from his subjects and Henry, understanding Anne's meaning,
attempted to defend his chief minister, saying 'as for that, there
is in him no blame. For I know that matter better than you or
any other'. Anne was not to be beaten however and she replied
that Wolsey had done enough to warrant his execution. Henry
then responded sadly that he perceived that Anne was 'not the
cardinal's friend'. Anne agreed saying 'I have no cause to be.
Nor hath any other man that loves your Grace. No more has
your Grace, if ye consider well his doings'.

Anne succeeded in planting a seed of doubt in Henry's mind
and both she and her followers worked hard to ensure that
Wolsey was not granted access to the king. The morning after
Anne's discussion at dinner with the king, Wolsey arrived at
court for a meeting with Henry but he found the king ready
to ride and unable to see him. When Wolsey asked the cause
of this, he was told that Anne had arranged to keep the king
busy all day and had provided a picnic to ensure that they
would not return before the Cardinal had gone. This may
have been the first moment that Wolsey perceived just how
powerful an enemy he had in Anne, exactly as Anne herself
would have wished. Wolsey and Campeggio both left court
that day, with Campeggio returning to Rome. Wolsey would
never see Henry VIII again.

Wolsey was certainly right to be concerned about Henry's
opinion of him and, when Cardinal Campeggio reached
Calais, he was stopped on Henry's orders while his bags were
searched on the suspicion that he was carrying money to
facilitate Wolsey's flight to Rome. Campeggio was found to
be carrying nothing but the news of the search must have filled
Wolsey with dread. He certainly had reason to be fearful and,
on 9 October 1529, he was charged with taking orders from a
foreign power (i.e. the Pope) and forced to surrender the great
seal and his position as chancellor. Wolsey was ordered to
retire to Esher but he was not arrested. He quickly surrendered
all his possessions to the king and threw himself on Henry's
mercy. Wolsey knew that the best way to assuage Henry's anger
was by appealing to the king's greed and before he left his own
house he 'called all the officers of his household before him,
to take account of all such stuff as they had in their charge.

And in his gallery there were set divers tables, whereupon were laid a great number of rich stuffs'. In Wolsey's chambers adjoining the gallery further tables were set up to display his fine plate and other goods. A few days later Henry and Anne travelled secretly to York Place to view their new possessions and Anne must have felt triumphant to know that all that the Cardinal had once owned now belonged to both her and the king. Wolsey was forced to stay in a borrowed house at Esher making use of borrowed dishes, plate and cloth.

Although he had fallen from power, Wolsey still had hopes of a return to favour, as he explained to William Cavendish one evening:

'By my submission, the king, I doubt not, had a great remorse of conscience, wherein he would rather pity me than malign me. And also there was a continual serpentine enemy about the king who would, I am well assured, if I had been found stiff necked, have called continually upon the king in his ear (I mean the night-crow) with such a vehemency that I should with the help of her assistance have obtained sooner the king's indignation than his lawful favour'.

Wolsey fully recognised the role that Anne had played in his fall and his nickname of her as the 'night-crow' was intended to be very far from flattering. His hopes of a return to favour seemed very real to Anne in late 1529 and early 1530 and there were signs that Henry had not entirely forgotten his fallen favourite. At Christmas 1529, for example, Wolsey fell sick and Henry sent his own physician to attend him. Henry also insisted that Anne send a token of comfort to the Cardinal, something that must have struck terror into Anne's heart, although she complied by sending a gold tablet. For Candlemas that year, Henry sent Wolsey four cart loads of gifts, another sign of a possible return to favour.

Henry had not entirely abandoned Wolsey but he still refused to see him, leaving Anne in a position to continue to undermine the Cardinal's influence. Both Anne and her uncle, the Duke of Norfolk, worked continually on Henry to persuade him to send the Cardinal away and, finally, at Easter 1530 Wolsey was ordered to travel north to his diocese of York. Although Wolsey made his journey something of a triumphal progress, he would have been aware, as was Anne, that his removal to the north would take him fully out of the king's thoughts and favour.

Wolsey was staying at Cawood in the north of England in November 1530 when the Earl of Northumberland and a

Master Walsh arrived one evening to arrest him. Anne's hand can be seen in the choice of Northumberland as the agent of Wolsey's arrest and both she and Wolsey would have been aware that the Earl was her former suitor, Henry Percy. Anne must have felt that it was fitting that Percy should exercise the final revenge on Wolsey for the breaking of their engagement. If this was the case she had misjudged Percy and he did not relish his role. Wolsey was at first unaware of the reason for Percy's arrival and he took Percy to his bedchamber:

> 'The earl, trembling, said with a very faint and soft voice unto my lord, laying his hand upon his arm, "My lord", quoth he, "I arrest you of high treason". With which words my lord was marvellously astonished, the two of them standing still a long space without any further words. But at last, quoth my lord, "what moveth you, or by what authority do you this?"'

Percy said that he had a commission but that he was not permitted to allow Wolsey to see it. Wolsey then refused to allow Percy to arrest him, submitting only to Master Walsh. Anne must have been angered to hear of Wolsey's conduct at his arrest in refusing to submit to Percy. There was much speculation about this as to 'whether hee did out of stubbornesse to the Erle, who had been heretofore educated in his house, or out of despight to Mistris Anne Bolen, who (he might conceive) had put this affront upon him, in finding means to employ her Antient Suitor to take Revenge in both their names'. She would have known, as Wolsey did, that his defiance was only an empty gesture.

Following his arrest, Wolsey was taken towards London with his legs tied to his horse. He was a broken man and full of remorse, stating that 'had I serv'd God as diligently as I had done the King, hee would not have given me over, in my gray haires; but this is my just reward'. Wolsey did not make it as far as London, where he faced trial and execution. He died at Leicester on 29 November 1530. It was suggested that he took poison to avoid a more shameful death although he may also simply have died an old and broken man, aware that his fall from grace was to be made permanent.

Anne Boleyn cannot but have rejoiced at news of Cardinal Wolsey's death. He had never been a friend to her and, at times, he had actively worked against her. She pursued her grudge against him for over eight years and she must have felt both relief and jubilation once the threat of his return to power had passed. The power that Anne wielded in bringing about the fall of Wolsey also demonstrated to her just how great her hold over the king was. By the end of 1530, Anne Boleyn was queen in all but name although she can never have imagined just how much longer she would have to wait before she could finally truly claim the role as her own.

CHAPTER 9

The Concubine

By the time of Wolsey's death, Anne had become the most powerful person at court after the king. In a way, she was his first minister and she quickly set about adopting the trappings and manners of queenship just as Wolsey, in his turn, had made himself a prince of the Church. One thing continued to elude her in the years between 1530 and 1532 and that was the title of queen itself. For both Anne and Henry, the years 1530 to 1532 were a time of stagnation and disappointed hopes but slowly they were able to move towards their ultimate goal.

In the early years of the King's Great Matter, Anne had often absented herself from court, keeping in the background as much as possible so that blame for Henry's treatment of his wife and daughter did not fall on her. As the years wore on, the couple grew increasingly frustrated with Henry's continued marriage to Catherine and it was soon apparent to everyone that Henry was alienating himself from the queen and that Anne was quickly taking her place. Anne was no longer expected to serve the queen even nominally, and by late 1528 she had been given her own lodging at court in rooms that were amongst the finest at court. Anne was thrilled by this proof of Henry's commitment to her and she always loved playing the role of queen. According to the French ambassador, even as early as December 1528 'greater court is now paid to her every day than has been to the Queen for a long time. I see they mean to accustom the people by degrees to endure her, so that when the great blow comes it may not be thought strange'. Anne revelled in her role as an almost-queen and, as the years went on, she came to develop an imperious nature to fit her new found status.

Anne had always had a fiery and impetuous temper and this was certainly part of the attraction to Henry. With the years of frustration, Anne often let her temper get the better of her and she alienated many of the great men at court, including members of her own family. While Anne's behaviour was imperious and often unreasonable, she was in a very difficult position and her patience must often have been sorely tried. She also saw herself as the rightful queen and expected to be obeyed as such, regardless of what anyone else thought. Flushed with success from the fall of Wolsey, Anne was not prepared to tolerate any discourtesies or slights towards her.

Anne's disagreements with members of the court were notorious and she fell out with her uncle, the Duke of Norfolk, in early 1530. Norfolk was angry with the lack of respect his niece showed to him, but held his tongue for the time being, seeing the benefits in keeping Anne friendly. However, by mid 1531 there were rumours that he had left the court due to a dispute with his niece. Anne, secure in the king's love, was not afraid to offend anybody and she reasoned that there was little harm they could do her in her exalted position. Anne also made an enemy of her aunt, the Duchess of Norfolk. The Duchess had probably always disliked her niece and was a staunch supporter of Queen Catherine, telling the queen when Anne attempted to recruit her to her cause that 'if all the world were to try it she would remain faithful to her [Catherine]. She also desired the queen to be of good courage, for her opponents were at their wits' end, being further off from their object than the day they began'. Anne was in no mood to tolerate family disloyalty and, at Anne's request, the Duchess was sent home from court 'because she spoke too freely, and declared herself more than they liked for the queen'. Anne also quarrelled with her father in the summer of 1532 when he asked her to intercede for the life of a young priest condemned for clipping coins. Anne, in typically outspoken manner, 'told her father that he did wrong to speak for a priest as there were too many of them already'.

The uncertainty of her position made Anne sensitive to any perceived slight and wherever she went at court there would have been whispered conversations when she entered the room and strange looks. Although Anne was often arbitrary and over-sensitive in her behaviour, for much of the time between 1530 and 1532 she was on edge, aware of the disapproval that she garnered at court, for all her attempts to ignore it. One person who earned Anne's enmity was the controller of Henry's household. According to the imperial ambassador,

Eustace Chapuys, who is a useful, if hardly an impartial, source:

> 'The Lady, knowing that Guildford, the controller, was not very partial to her, has threatened him bravely, going so far as to say that when she is queen she will deprive him of his office. To which he replied, that when that time arrived, she should have no trouble to deprive him, for he would give up his office himself. He then went to the king to tell him the story, and give up at once the baton of his office, - which the king restored to him twice, saying he should not trouble himself with what women said. The Controller, however, has, from disgust or for some other reason, gone to his house'.

Henry may also have received the sharp end of Anne's tongue when she heard of this exchange and she was not afraid to angrily berate the king when she did not get her own way. Anne's independence was a large part of her attraction to the king but, as the divorce dragged on, their relationship became increasingly stormy. Anne, as her frustration mounted, often found it difficult to remain even-tempered with Henry, particularly as it was she, rather than the king, who had to bear the brunt of the whispering and rumours that surrounded their relationship. According to Chapuys, in November 1530, Anne and Henry had a public argument about Cardinal Wolsey to the interest and embarrassment of the court. According to the ambassador, Anne:

> 'Does not cease to weep and regret her lost honour, threatening the king that she would leave him, in such sort that the king has had much trouble to appease her; and though the king prayed her most affectionately, even with tears in his eyes, that she would not speak of leaving him, nothing could satisfy her except the arrest of the Cardinal'.

Henry was so besotted with Anne that she had the power to bring him publicly to tears. The arguments never lasted and once they were reconciled the couple appeared even more in love to everyone at court than before. Even Henry sometimes became frustrated and complained to Norfolk that Anne was 'not like the Queen, who had never in her life used ill words to him'. Norfolk certainly agreed and privately said that Anne would be the ruin of all her family. Henry always made amends and in early 1531 a report reached Rome that Henry had desperately summoned some of Anne's relatives to court to beg them in tears to help him make his peace with Anne.

Henry frequently made a public fool of himself in his fervour for Anne and his love for her was all that mattered. Henry's obvious devotion and her own feelings for him must have helped ensure that the disagreements were always short-lived and Anne reserved the bulk of her anger and ill feeling for Catherine of Aragon and her daughter, Princess Mary.

Anne Boleyn's behaviour towards Catherine and Mary shows her character in the worst possible light and there is no doubt that she was guilty of great cruelty towards the pair. It is difficult to defend her conduct but she was in a very difficult situation. Anne had been one of Catherine's ladies, but she is unlikely to have had a personal relationship with the queen. She may have barely known Catherine and her daughter and, when the opportunity to become queen presented itself, she had no personal feelings of loyalty towards the king's current wife. As the years dragged on and Catherine proved so intractable, Anne's frustration with the women, as the barrier to her own happiness, would have become acute, and it is clear that she came to hate them as the two people who stood in the way of her greatest ambition. Cardinal Wolsey had been Anne's greatest enemy, but he was soon supplanted by Catherine of Aragon in Anne's hatred and the two women were implacably opposed.

Eustace Chapuys, the Imperial ambassador, and one of Catherine's greatest supporters, chronicled the difficult relationship between the two women and, although his accounts are entirely partisan, always referring to Anne either as 'the Lady' or 'the Concubine', they provide a useful source for just how frustrated and angry Anne had become with her rival's intransigence. According to Chapuys, by Christmas 1530, Anne was certain that her marriage would soon be accomplished:

'She is braver than a lion. She said to one of the Queen's ladies that she wished all the Spaniards in the world were in the sea; and on the other replying, that, for the honour of the Queen, she should not say so, she said that she did not care anything for the Queen, and would rather see her hanged than acknowledge her as her mistress'.

This was a truly shocking thing for any woman to say and again shows Anne's independent spirit. Anne could not afford to have any sympathy for Catherine's position and she was implacable in her hatred of her. Anne used many of the same tactics with Catherine that she had used so effectively on Wolsey and she pursued a policy of keeping the king away from his wife, encouraging Henry not to visit Catherine or see her when they were together at court. Anne also commented that York Place was her favourite palace and that she liked 'better that the king should stay in the said house than elsewhere, as there is no lodging in it for the queen'. It must have been particularly galling for Anne to recognise just how formidable an enemy Catherine of Aragon was and as Anne's own uncle, Norfolk, commented with grudging admiration, the queen's 'courage was supernatural'.

Throughout the years of the divorce, Catherine fought to maintain her position as queen and as Henry's wife. For several years this policy was successful and, up until mid 1531 Henry, Anne and Catherine presented an odd group as they spent most of the time confined together within the court. Although Henry was still insisting that his marriage was invalid, he did not allow this to interrupt the routine of the court and, for the most part, Catherine was still queen in deed as well as name. Henry even went so far as to continue to request that Catherine make his shirts for him, something that infuriated Anne when she found out. Henry and Catherine also still dined together as husband and wife well into 1531 and appear to have been able to have a civilised conversation, for all the animosity that they must have felt for each other. According to Chapuys, at one such meal in May 1531:

'The King, dining the other day with the Queen, as is usual in most festivals, began to speak of the Turk and the truce concluded with your Majesty [Charles V], praising your puissance, contrary to his wont. Afterward proceeding to speak of the Princess, he accused the Queen of cruelty, because she had not made her physician reside continually with her; and so the dinner passed amicably. Next day, when the Queen, in consequence of these gracious speeches, asked the King to allow the Princess to see them, he rebuffed her very rudely, and said she might go and see the Princess if she wished, and also stop there. The Queen graciously replied that she would not leave him for her daughter nor any one else in the world'.

Both Anne and Henry knew that Catherine would never leave the king regardless of how cruelly he behaved towards her. Anne, who often proved more decisive than Henry, could not endure this situation and she continually berated the king about his failure to take action to separate from his wife and commit fully to their own future marriage. The pressure Anne put on Henry finally bore fruit and on 11 July 1531 Anne and Henry secretly left Windsor with a small retinue of followers, leaving Catherine behind. Anne felt exhilarated as she rode away with the king, knowing that suddenly, everything had changed.

Catherine on the other hand was bewildered by Henry's disappearance. By custom, she and Henry had been in the habit of visiting each other every three days and when Henry had not returned after six days she sent him a message asking after his health and 'to tell him of the concern she felt in not having been able to speak with him at his departure'. Henry was furious to receive her message and recalling her messenger:

> 'In great choler and anger, as it seemed, charged him to tell the Queen that he had no need to bid her adieu, nor to give her that consolation of which she spoke, nor any other, and still less that she should send to visit him, or to inquire of his estate; that she had given him occasion to speak such things, and that he was sorry and angry at her because she had wished to bring shame upon him by having him personally cited [to appear in Rome]; and still more, she had refused (like an obstinate woman as she was) the just and reasonable request made by his Council and other nobles of his realm'.

Henry was used to getting his own way and no one had ever defied him like Catherine had. Catherine, undaunted, sent another message and Henry replied banning her from sending him any messages or anything else, stating that he did not consider himself her husband. Catherine could not have known it but on the 11 July Anne had won and Henry and Catherine were never to meet or correspond directly with each other again. Most people in England assumed that Henry's final rejection of Catherine was the work of Anne, and Chapuys commented of Henry's last letter to Catherine that 'it may be supposed, considering the Lady's authority, and the good reason contained in the said letter, that she must have dictated it'. Anne was commonly held to be the driving force behind the king's desire to be rid of Catherine and she was hated for it.

Following Henry's abandonment of Catherine, he also commanded the queen to separate from her daughter and the two women were never to see each other again. This was also widely held to be Anne's doing and in April 1531 a request made by Mary to join her parents was refused by the king. According to Chapuys, this was refused by the king in order to please Anne 'who hates her as much as the queen, or more so, chiefly because she sees the king has some affection for her'. There is no doubt that Anne hated Mary and behaved cruelly to the teenaged princess, even ensuring that her spies were present when Mary and Henry met in order that the conversation would be reported back to her. Anne's treatment of Mary is almost indefensible but, once again, she would have had no personal feelings for Mary and probably saw her only as an obstinate girl who stood in the way of her greatest desire. Once she became queen, she also knew that Mary would have to be broken to ensure that she was no threat to Anne's own children.

Anne's unpopularity probably took her by surprise. Catherine had been queen of England for nearly twenty years by the time the king first raised the issue of divorce and both she and Mary were loved. Anne, on the other hand, was seen as an upstart and an immoral woman. Even as early as December 1528, when Henry began to try to condition the people to accept Anne, the French ambassador reported that 'the people remain quite hardened, and I think they would do more if they had more power'. Throughout the divorce there were mutterings against Anne Boleyn and the majority of people in England never came to love her. Anne was angered by the hostility towards her, and furious at the rumours that surrounded her. She was widely reputed to be the king's mistress, with regular reports that she was pregnant or already the mother of the king's child. Anne always adopted a public facade of indifference to the hostility and rumours, but some rumours were difficult to ignore.

John Fisher, Bishop of Rochester, had spoken in defence of Catherine's marriage at the Blackfriars trial and he remained a passionate supporter of the queen, much to both Anne and Henry's anger. Fisher was in his London house one day in February 1531 when he decided not to eat his dinner as he was too engrossed in studying. The rest of his household sat down to dinner, eating the same meal that had been prepared for Fisher. Soon after the meal, all those who had eaten the pottage prepared fell ill and two members of the household died. It was clear to everyone that the pottage had been poisoned and the cook confessed that he had thrown a mysterious white powder into the food as it cooked. Henry immediately ordered that the cook was boiled alive as an example to all poisoners. According to Chapuys, 'the king has done well to show dissatisfaction at this; nevertheless he cannot wholly avoid suspicion, if not against himself, whom I think too good to do such a thing, at least against the lady and her father'. Chapuys' view was widely held across England and

Fisher believed that the Boleyns were behind the attempt on his life. According to Fisher's biographer, it was also not the only attempt to murder Fisher and a canon was shot at his house soon after the attempt to poison him. The shot narrowly missed him, damaging the roof of his house. A search was made and the gun was found to have been shot from a house belonging to Thomas Boleyn. Two attempts on his life were enough for Fisher and perceiving 'that great malice was ment towards him' he left London for Rochester. Anne, for all her bluster, was no murderess. There is no evidence that she ever attempted to murder Wolsey or Catherine or Mary and she would certainly not have risked her position merely to bring down John Fisher. The story does show just how poorly Anne was perceived by the people of England and that anything could be believed of her.

Anne always tried to ignore the bad feeling shown towards her by the people of England. In the summer of 1532, for example, she and Henry were forced to turn back from a hunting trip as wherever they went the people lined the streets urging Henry to take back Catherine. The women, in particular reserved their ire for Anne and insulted her. Anne was always careful to show that she did not care and she probably put many of the reactions down to jealousy. By mid 1532, she was the sole woman in the king's life and she would have known that her marriage was only a matter of time.

Catherine had continued to press her nephew and the Pope for a judgment in favour of her marriage but Clement VII vacillated, unwilling to pronounce either way and risk a rift with either the emperor or Henry. By mid 1532, both Henry and Anne had realised that the Pope would never grant the divorce and finally Henry decided to take more decisive action. Anne was already fulfilling most of the role of queen by that stage. In 1529, Thomas Boleyn had been created Earl of Wiltshire and Ormond and at the banquet to celebrate the appointment, Anne took the place of the queen. Although this event gave Anne the title of Lady Anne Rochford, it was still not enough for Anne and, in September 1532, Henry decided to take the unprecedented step of creating her a peeress in her own right. On 1 September Anne knelt before Henry as he created her Lady Marquis of Pembroke with land grants worth one thousand pounds a year. It is of particular note that in the patent conferring the title on Anne, the title and lands were stated to descend to her male heirs, rather than the more usual specification that it must be legitimate male heirs. This is a clear indication of a change in the nature of Anne and

Henry's relationship and it indicates that they were close to consummating their relationship.

Due to her upbringing in France, Anne was always in favour of a French alliance and worked closely with the French ambassadors. Given his difficulties with the emperor, Henry was also in favour of a French alliance and, on 10 October 1532, Anne and Henry travelled to Dover, sailing to Calais the next day. The meeting with Francis was intended to be Anne's Field of the Cloth of Gold, introducing her to the world as the next queen of England and before the journey Anne was busy buying costly dresses to ensure that she looked the part. Henry also wanted to show Anne's suitability as queen to the world and:

> 'The king, not contented with having given her [Anne] his jewels, sent the Duke of Norfolk to obtain the Queen's as well. She replied that she could not send jewels or anything else to the king, as he had long ago forbidden her to do so; and, besides, it was against her conscience to give her jewels to adorn a person who is the scandal of Christendom, and a disgrace to the king, who takes her to such an assembly; however, if the king sent expressly to ask for them, she would obey him in this as in other things'.

Henry was angered by Catherine's response, but he sent to her expressly and Anne may have been wearing some of Catherine's jewels when she first set foot in France after over ten years away. The visit was always intended to be Anne's triumph, but it was, of necessity, a smaller occasion than the Field of the Cloth of Gold. Although Anne was a queen in all but name by late 1532, she still was not actually queen. Francis's new wife, Eleanor of Austria, was the sister of the emperor and so would never have been expected by Anne to attend. Both Anne and Henry had hopes that Francis's sister Marguerite would agree to meet Anne and they were deeply disappointed when she also refused. Francis offered his mistress, the Duchess of Vendome, but this simply would not do and it was finally agreed that there would be no French ladies in the party. Anne therefore waited at Calais when Henry rode to meet Francis. She was placated by the enormous diamond Francis sent her on her arrival.

Henry spent several days with Francis before bringing the French king back to Calais with him and Anne spent that time preparing for her first meeting with Francis in a decade. Both she and Henry ensured that England was displayed in its greatest splendour to the French king and his lodging in Calais was hung with satin silk and silver with a carpet of cloth of gold embroidered with flowers. Henry then hosted a great banquet in Francis's honour whilst Anne prepared excitedly for her big moment. According to Hall's Chronicle:

'After supper came in the Marchioness of Pembroke, with vii ladies in masking apparel, of straunge fashion, made of clothe of gold, compassed with crimosyn tinsell satin, owned with clothe of silver, lying lose and knit with laces of gold; these ladies were brought into the chamber, with the four damoselles apparelled in crimosin sattyn, with tabards of fine cipres: the lady Marqyes tooke the Frenche kyng, and the Countes of Darby, toke the King of Naver, and every lady toke a lorde, and in daunsyng the kyng of Englande, toke awaie the ladies visers, so that there the ladies beauties were shewed, and after they had daunsed a while they ceased, and the French kyng talked with the Marchioness of Pembroke a pace, & then he toke his leave of the ladies, and the kyng conveighed hym to his lodgyng'.

Anne's meeting with Francis was an unqualified success and they perhaps reminisced about the old days when they had known each other in France. For both Anne and Henry, Francis's approval was the recognition they needed and they finally consummated their relationship for the first time. This may have been as they waited at Calais for several weeks for the weather to change and it is a testament to the security that Anne finally felt in her relationship with Henry. She would be his wife and she would be his queen and, in late 1532, she knew that it would be only a matter of months.

There had been rumours that Anne and Henry would marry in France, although Anne had insisted that 'even if the King wished, she would not consent, for she wished it to be done here in the place where queens are wont to be married and crowned'. By late 1532, Anne was secure enough to make demands about what her marriage would be and in January she knew that she was more secure still. By the middle of January, Anne would have been certain that she was pregnant. This was no longer the disaster that it could earlier have been and, on 25 January, Anne and Henry came quietly to Whitehall attended only by Henry Norris and Mr Henage of Henry's privy chamber and Anne's friend, Lady Berkeley. Henry's chaplain, Rowland Lee, was also summoned and married the couple secretly, receiving the office of Bishop of Lichfield for his pains.

Few details survive of Anne and Henry's marriage and it was kept secret even from their closest supporters. For Henry, it was probably the happiest moment of his life and for Anne, it was her moment of triumph. Anne left the ceremony glowing with happiness, secure in the knowledge that she was now the king's wife. She would have been very aware that, while she was the king's wife, she was not yet his queen and that Henry was still firmly married to Catherine of Aragon.

CHAPTER 10

Pope in England

In January 1533, Anne was finally married to the king and expecting his child. In spite of this, there was still a great deal of work to do to ensure that she was recognised as both Henry's wife and his queen and the fact of her pregnancy meant that the clock was rapidly ticking away. Anne was at her happiest in early 1533, knowing that everything was at last going as she had planned. However, in order to finally achieve the divorce, both Henry and Anne had to engineer a radical solution that changed England forever.

In the early months of 1533 Henry and Anne knew that they had to keep their marriage secret to ensure that no word of it reached the Pope or the emperor. Anne was triumphant and neither she nor Henry could refrain from dropping hints about her altered state. It must have amused Anne to see the confusion on people's faces as she spoke of her marriage and pregnancy and the shock she caused. On one occasion in February, while dining in her chamber with some members of the court, Anne could not resist saying, several times that 'she felt as sure as death that the king would marry her shortly'. Anne's indiscretion continued and, shortly after this incident, Anne informed stunned observers that she had developed a craving for apples and that the king had told her this was a sign that she was pregnant. Coming from the supposedly unmarried Anne, these hints were shocking, but Anne simply did not care. She knew that she was married and, once the king's divorce was finally out of the way, she could declare it to the world. Henry was also as committed to their marriage as ever and, in early March, he dropped hints of the marriage to Anne's step-grandmother, the Dowager Duchess of Norfolk. According to Chapuys, during a banquet in Anne's chamber,

Henry pointed out Anne's rich possessions and referred to her rich marriage. Anne and Henry must have shared a smile during the meal over their secret although they would have been aware that most people at court suspected the truth. Even Catherine, kept in exile away from London, knew that there was some new plot against her. Catherine was fearful that the sudden promotion of the unknown Thomas Cranmer to the see of Canterbury 'was for the purpose of attempting something against her'. She was, of course, correct.

Henry had always preferred to secure his divorce through a sentence given by the Pope but, as the years dragged on, it became necessary to consider other solutions. Many in England always believed that Anne was the driving force behind the break with Rome. Chapuys, on one occasion, described Anne and her father as 'more Lutheran than Luther himself'. This is an exaggeration, but there is no doubt that Anne, and her brother and father, were very interested in the religious reform movement. For Anne, her interest lay in the reformer's promotion of the scriptures in the vernacular language, rather than Latin, as set out by William Tyndale, one of the main English reformers in 1526:

> 'Moreover, because the kingdom of heaven, which is the Scripture and Word of God, may be so locked up, that he which readeth or heareth it cannot understand it; as Christ testifieth how that the scribes and Pharisees had so shut it up and had taken away the key of knowledge that their Jews which thought themselves within, were yet so locked out, and are to this day that they can understand no sentence of the Scripture unto their salvation, though they can rehearse the texts everywhere and dispute thereof as subtly as the Popish doctors of dunce's dark learning, which with their sophistry, served us, as the Pharisees do the Jews'.

Anne owned a copy of the Bible in French and later kept an English version on display, signifying her reformist beliefs. She was certainly not a fully fledged Protestant and statements she later made in the Tower demonstrate that she did not accept the key Protestant doctrine of justification by faith alone. However, she was certainly anti-papal and she worked hard to ensure that Henry also became interested in the movement.

Anne's reputation as a reformer was well known both in England and on the Continent and a number of reformist scholars presented her with copies of their works. Anne obtained a copy of Tyndale's *Obedience of a Christian Man*, which had so upset Wolsey, early in her relationship with

Henry and she marked out passages that she thought would be of interest to him. Anne also possessed Simon Fish's anti-clerical work, *The Supplication of Beggars,* which criticised the cult of purgatory and the payment of ecclesiastical fees. More pertinently, for Anne, Fish argued that the king's laws could not be enforced against the Pope's as the chancellor was generally a priest. No one else had ever dared show Henry such 'heretical' works before, but Anne did and, gradually, as the divorce dragged on, she was able to persuade the king to take an increasingly anti-papal stance. Anne was also supported in this by Thomas Cromwell, a lawyer who was rising fast in Henry's service and shared her reformist views.

Anne was always given credit as a major architect behind the reformation and Foxe, in his *Acts and Monuments,* claimed that she was almost its sole architect. According to Foxe:

> 'It was touched, a little before, how the pope had lost great part of his authority and jurisdiction in this realm of England; now it followeth to infer, how and by what occasion his whole power and authority began utterly to be abolished by the reason and occasion of the most virtuous and noble lady, Anne Bullen, who was not as yet married to the king, howbeit in great favour: by whose godly means and most virtuous counsel the king's mind was daily inclined better and better. Insomuch that, not long after, the king, belike perceiving the minds of the clergy not much favouring his cause, sent for the speaker again, and twelve of the common-house, having with him eight lords, and said to them, "Well-beloved subjects: we had thought the clergy of our realm had been our subjects wholly, but now we have well perceived that they be but half our subjects, yea and scarce our subjects. For all the prelates at their consecration make an oath to the pope, clean contrary to the oath that they make unto us, so that they seem to be his subjects, and not ours'.

Whilst Foxe's favourable account of Anne is as much propaganda as the more hostile accounts, it contains an element of truth. Anne was always inclined towards religious reform and she saw a means by which these views could be useful to the divorce.

Henry's first move against the Pope occurred in the praemunire manoeuvres of 1531. In the summer of 1530, fifteen clerics and one lay proctor were prosecuted by Henry for prioritising papal law over that of the king. This case was quickly postponed and, during the autumn and winter of 1530, it was extended by Thomas Cromwell, working closely with the king, into an attack on the entire southern clergy.

In January 1531, when the clergy met in convocation, Henry insisted that they purchase a pardon for praemunire from him for £100,000. After some debate, the clergy agreed to pay this sum to the king on 24 January 1531 but Henry was not finished with the clergy. On 7 February he sent a document containing five articles to the clergy which he required them to accept. The first article was that the clergy recognise him as sole protector and supreme head of the Church in England.

Henry regarded this title as a fact to be confirmed, rather than something that he hoped to achieve but, for the clergy, it was an unheard of thing to ask and they debated for some time. Finally, a compromise was reached on 11 February where the clergy agreed to acknowledge Henry as 'Supreme Head of the Church of England, as far as the law of Christ allows'. This qualification rendered the title virtually meaningless but, for Henry and Anne, it was certainly a start in their moves against the Pope. That Henry should even have attempted such a thing shocked his contemporaries and Chapuys reported that 'the clergy have been compelled, under pain of the said law of praemunire, to accept the king as head of the Church, which implies in effect as much as if they had declared him Pope in England'. Anne was thrilled at the step towards reform and divorce and she showed herself 'as much delighted as if she had gained paradise'. For Anne, the praemunire manoeuvres were a sign that she soon would do.

Following the praemunire manoeuvres of early 1531, Henry became increasingly anti-papal in his outlook, supported by both Anne and her father. In 1531 and 1532, Henry was still attempting to persuade the pope to grant him a divorce and, while Anne and Thomas Boleyn may have hoped that Henry's actions were a step towards reform, for Henry they were probably intended only to push the Pope into taking action on his behalf. Certainly, following the praemunire manoeuvres, advocates of the reform became more open about their beliefs in England. In March 1531, for example, a Lutheran preacher who was sentenced to be burned, insisted that he should be tried again by secular persons and both Norfolk and Thomas Boleyn were sent to interrogate him. Given the involvement of Thomas Boleyn, it is likely that it was Anne herself who persuaded Henry to see the preacher. When he was brought before Henry, he was presented with a roll containing the articles of his heresy. Henry read them and noticed that the first item was that the preacher had claimed that the Pope was not the Head of the Christian Church. At this, Henry said that 'that ought not to be entered among the heresies, for it was quite certain and true'. Henry then released him. Chapuys believed that it was Anne's influence that had secured the preacher's release and he may be right. It is also clear that Anne's influence was changing the opinions of the king and, in May 1532, Henry permitted a preacher to openly assert that the Pope was a heretic, something which was again attributed to the influence of Anne and Thomas Boleyn.

Throughout 1531 and 1532, Henry continued in his attempts to goad the pope into action. In early 1532, for example, he caused an Act for the Conditional Restraint of Annates to be passed by parliament. Annates were the first year of revenue belonging to the see of a newly appointed bishop and, traditionally, they were paid to the Pope. This could involve quite considerable sums and it is certain that Clement VII was anxious about the loss of this revenue. For Henry, this was a radical move and is testament to his frustration with the papacy. For Anne, Henry's moves against the papacy must have seemed agonisingly slow and she constantly pushed Henry to take more decisive action. As the *Life of Fisher*, for example, notes:

> 'She was greatly suspected, and in a manner notoriously knowne of divers persons to be an heretick, and therby verie likely to corrupt the kinge, being so extreamely blinded with their unlawfull doctrine as she was, which after came to passe in deed: for she was the only person that of a longe time durst break with him in such matters'.

Anne was the only person who dared urge Henry on towards a break with Rome and her pregnancy and secret marriage in early 1533 meant that a solution urgently had to be found. The death of the conservative and aged William Warham, Archbishop of Canterbury, in August 1532 provided them with the perfect opportunity to secure the divorce.

Henry had inherited Warham from his father and both he and Anne knew that the conservative archbishop was unlikely to be amenable to the radical solution that they had in mind. His death secured the way for a more reform-minded successor and the choice quickly fell to the unknown Thomas Cranmer. Cranmer had been appointed as one of the king's chaplains in January 1532, almost certainly on Anne's recommendation. He had previously been a member of Thomas Boleyn's household and would have got to know Anne well during that period. Most importantly for both Anne and Henry, he also held strong reformist views and was, in fact, already secretly married when he accepted the post of Archbishop of Canterbury early in 1533. As soon as he was appointed, a request was made to the pope for the bulls confirming Cranmer's appointment and Clement, anxious to do anything to appease Henry, unsuspectingly dispatched them in March 1533. Soon after they arrived, Cranmer repudiated his oath of loyalty to the Pope, allowing both Anne and Henry to be confident that the divorce was imminent.

The major difficulty in obtaining the divorce had always been that Catherine, rather than allowing the case to be heard in England, had appealed to Rome. This was, of course, an entirely rational step for the queen to take, but for Henry and Anne it was infuriating. With the appointment of Cranmer, a more amenable Archbishop, it became imperative for Anne and Henry that the case be heard in England and in February 1533 an Act in Restraint of Appeals was passed rapidly in parliament. This was the last statute needed to engineer both the king's divorce and the break with Rome and the wording of the Act was a clear statement of the way in which the king's title of Supreme Head of the Church was now to be interpreted:

'Where by divers sundry old authentic histories and chronicles it is manifestly declared and expressed that this realm of England is an empire, and so hath been accepted in the world, governed by one supreme head and king, having the dignity and royal estate of the imperial crown of the same, unto whom a body politic, compact of all sorts and degrees of people divided in terms and by names of spirituality and temporality, be bounden and ought to bear next to God, a natural and humble obedience, he being also institute and furnished by the goodness and sufferance of Almighty God with plenary, whole and entire power, pre-eminence, authority, prerogative and jurisdiction, to render and yield within this his realm, in all causes, matters, debates and contentious happenings to occur, insurge or begin within the limits thereof'.

The Act expressly stated that matrimonial causes should not be tried by appeal to Rome and that they must be heard within the Church of England. This was the final key statute required and, as soon as Cranmer's appointment was confirmed, he was ordered by the king to try the validity of Henry's marriage with Catherine.

In early May 1533, Cranmer travelled to Dunstable, four miles away from Catherine's residence at Ampthill. Cranmer immediately summoned the queen to attend a church court in order to try the validity of her marriage. Catherine, understandably, refused to heed the summons, saying 'that inasmuch as her cause was before the Pope, she would have none other judge; and therefore would not take me [Cranmer] for a judge'. Cranmer would have expected this response and this had also been anticipated by Henry who had already given the archbishop orders to proceed with the court regardless of whether the queen attended. Cranmer did just that and, on 8 May, gave final sentence in the court claiming that it had never been possible for the pope to dispense the marriage of Catherine and Henry due to Catherine's marriage to Arthur. The marriage had therefore been invalid from the start, leaving Henry entirely free to contract another marriage. It is likely that it was Cranmer himself who informed Anne and Henry of his verdict and, as soon as the sentence was given, he hurried back to London in order to prepare for Anne's coronation.

Even after the divorce had been pronounced, Henry always showed a commitment to the break with Rome and this may have been due to Anne's continuing influence. In early 1534, Henry put the final touches to the statutes with the Act for the Submission of the Clergy and Restraint of Appeals and the Act of Supremacy. Both Acts ensured that all Henry's previous actions against the Pope were contained in statute, and the Act of Supremacy sums up Henry's own beliefs about his power over the Pope:

'Albeit the king's majesty justly and rightfully is and oweth to be the Supreme Head of the Church of England, and so is recognised by the clergy of this realm in their Convocations, yet nevertheless for corroboration and confirmation thereof, and for increase of virtue in Christ's religion within this realm of England, and to repress and extirp all errors, heresies, and other enormities and abuses heretofore used in the same; be it enacted by authority of this present Parliament, that the king our Sovereign Lord, his heirs and successors, kings of this realm, shall be taken, accept and reputed the only Supreme Head in earth of the Church of England'.

Anne had never been a friend of the Pope and the fact that the aims of the reform movement and Henry's divorce coincided must have filled her with joy.

Anne Boleyn played a major role in the reformation, by urging Henry on and by supplying him with reformist ideas. She would always have been pleased that her own advancement had coincided with the fall of the Pope in England, just as it had earlier led to the fall of the hated Wolsey. According to Henry's chancellor, Wriothesley, Henry commanded that

Above: 1. Blickling Hall, Norfolk. A seventeenth century house now stands on the site of Anne Boleyn's birthplace.

Right: 2. The Howard coat of arms over the gate at Framlingham Castle, Suffolk. Anne was always proud of her Howard blood and this connection raised her to the highest ranks of the nobility.

3. Anne Boleyn. Anne did not conform to contemporary ideals of beauty but her grace and wit set her apart from the other ladies of the court.

Above: 4. The Henry VIII Bedroom at Hever Castle, Anne's childhood home.

Right: 5. A replica of the rich clock given to Anne by Henry as a wedding present.

6. Hever Castle, Kent. Anne's childhood home.

7. Hever Castle, Kent. The early months of Henry and Anne's romance took place against the backdrop of the Bolyen family home.

8. The gardens of Hever Castle would have provided a romantic setting during visits paid to Anne by the king.

9. Thomas Boleyn's tomb brass. Thomas always used his children to further his ambitions.

10. The tomb of Anne's uncle, the third Duke of Norfolk. Anne's relationship with her uncle was fraught and he always considered that she would be the ruin of her family.

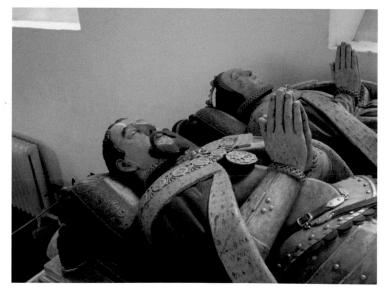

11. The tomb of Henry Howard, Earl of Surrey and his wife. Surrey was Anne's cousin and one of the peers who sat in judgment at her trial.

12. Henry VIII portrayed in all his magnificence at King's College, Cambridge.

13. Prince Arthur's Chamber at Ludlow Castle. The rooms in which Catherine of Aragon and Arthur spent their short married life.

14. Lady Margaret Beaufort above the gate at Christ's College, Cambridge. Henry's grandmother was an important example of a powerful royal woman and Anne attempted to follow the strict rules she laid down as to how a queen should behave.

15. The entwined initials of Anne and Henry displayed on the organ screen in King's College Chapel, Cambridge.

16. Anne Boleyn's falcon badge carved as graffiti into the wall of the Beauchamp Tower at the Tower of London.

Top: 17. Westminster Abbey. The site of Anne's greatest triumph when she was crowned queen of England. *Bottom:* The coronation procession of Anne Boleyn to Westminster Abbey, 31 May 1533.

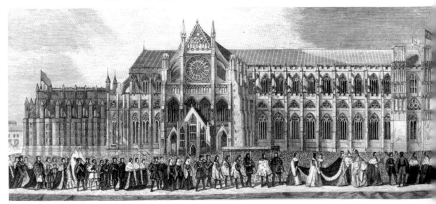

Top: 18. The Jewel Tower at Westminster Palace today. Little else remains of the palace that Anne knew. (Bottom) A view of Westminster about 1550 drawn by Anthony Van Wyngaerde.

19. Thomas Cranmer on his memorial at Oxford. Anne always considered Cranmer to be 'her' archbishop but at her fall he hurried to disassociate himself from her.

20. Hampton Court. The great palace which passed to Henry following the fall of Wolsey.

34. Henry VIII. Anne met the king when he was in his prime and the attraction between the couple is likely to have been mutual.

35. Thomas Wyatt. Anne enjoyed a flirtation with the poet but his marriage meant that their relationship could never advance to anything deeper.

Non secus ovnaa mari paulatim accrescit et alta
Neptum frontem supereminet; at sua tandem
Vis ruit, et pelago labens devoluitur imo,
Quam tua te WOLSEDE tumens evexit honoris
Aura, et sublimen super—exlusit ardua regis
Culmina, sed tandem conuerso CARDINE rerum,
In scopulos, rigidasq extrusa est gloria syrtes.
Terra olim corpus, tumuit, iam corpore tellus.

36. Cardinal Wolsey. Henry's chief minister and Anne's greatest enemy.

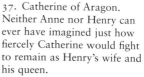

37. Catherine of Aragon. Neither Anne nor Henry can ever have imagined just how fiercely Catherine would fight to remain as Henry's wife and his queen.

38. Emperor Charles V. Catherine's nephew and a staunch supporter of her rights during the King's Great Matter.

39. Pope Clement VII. The Pope was kept as a virtual prisoner by the emperor and was never in a position to pronounce in favour of Henry's divorce.

40. William Warham, Archbishop of Canterbury. The death of the conservative archbishop cleared the way for the appointment of the more radical Thomas Cranmer.

41. Thomas Cranmer, Archbishop of Canterbury. Cranmer had been a chaplain of the Boleyn family and he shared their reformist ideals.

42. Thomas Cromwell. Henry's chief minister and one of the men responsible for Anne's fall.

43. Anne's daughter, Elizabeth I as queen. Anne was proud of her daughter and must have been fearful for Elizabeth's future following her arrest.

44. Mary Tudor, Henry's eldest daughter. Anne always saw Mary as a rival to her own daughter and was determined to crush her opposition.

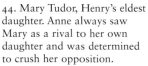

Tho. Moor L'Chancelour

45. Thomas More. Henry's chancellor died for his refusal to swear the Oath of Succession and so recognise the validity of Anne's marriage and the legitimacy of her children.

46. Jane Seymour. Anne's rival and successor as queen was coached on how to present a contrast to Anne to the king.

47. A nineteenth century illustration of the condemnation of Anne Boleyn showing the queen as a romantic heroine.

Left: 48. A nineteenth century representation of the execution of Anne Boleyn, 18 May, 1536.

Below: 49. A nineteenth century representation of Henry VIII and Anne Boleyn at Hever Castle in the days of their courtship.

50. Greenwich Palace c.1560 by Wyngaerde. Anne chose the palace for her lying in and gave birth to Princess Elizabeth there at 3pm on 7 September 1533.

51. London in c.1600. Little had changed in London in the sixty years after Anne's death and she knew it as a crowded and bustling city.

Above: 52. Letter from Anne Boleyn to Stephen Gardiner, then in Italy pursuing the king's quest for an annulment of his marriage. 4 April 1529.

Left: 53. One of a series of friendly letters which Anne Boleyn wrote to Cardinal Wolsey during the summer of 1528, when she was still looking to him as the man most likely to untangle the king's first marriage. She thanks him for the 'grete payne and trobell that yr grace doth take' about the matter (BL Cotton MS Vespasian F.XIII, f. 73.).

54. Henry VIII in about 1540 by Holbein.

ANNA BOLLINA ..... VXOR HEN VIII.

55. Anne Boleyn in a portrait belonging to Ripon Cathedral. It has recently been suggested that this is the most accurate depiction of Anne to survive.

all the bishops and curates in England 'should publishe and shewe to the people how the Pope hath usurped and taken upon him contrarie to Christen faythe, and that his authoritie and pardons should be extinct and putt downe out of this realme of England for ever more, and his name be blotted or putt out of the masse booke for ever'. Anne saw her marriage as leading to a great change for the better in England and, in April 1533, even before the divorce had actually been finally pronounced, Anne appeared publicly as queen for the first time. She was by then, not just Henry's wife, but also his queen.

CHAPTER 11

The Most Happy

Even before Henry's divorce from Catherine was pronounced, Anne and Henry knew that it would be necessary for them to openly declare their marriage to the world. Anne was anxious to be recognised as queen and both she and Henry wanted to ensure that their child would be legitimate. Henry's marriage to Anne was the public symbol of his break with Rome and he wanted to ensure the world recognised exactly what he had done.

Although Henry had still not secured the final pronouncement of his divorce, Anne and Henry decided to publicly announce their marriage on Easter Saturday 1533. By April Anne would have been noticeably pregnant and they may have felt that it was necessary to demonstrate the true nature of their relationship to ensure that their child was unquestionably legitimate. After six years of waiting, Anne was anxious to show herself to the world as the queen she had become and she made grand preparations for her appearance on Easter Saturday, intending to outshine Catherine and display herself as every inch the queen. Anne probably also gained a private satisfaction at the shock shown by Catherine's supporters at court and, certainly, Chapuys was astounded, writing:

'On Saturday, Easter Eve, dame Anne went to mass in Royal state, loaded with jewels, clothed in a robe of cloth of gold friese. The daughter of the Duke of Norfolk, who is affianced to the duke of Richmond, carried her train, and she had in her suite 60 young ladies, and was brought to church, and brought back again with the solemnities, or even more, which were used to the queen. She has changed her name from marchioness to Queen, and the preachers offered prayers for her by name. All the world is astonished at it, for it looks like a dream, and even those who take her part know not whether to laugh or to cry'.

Anne's first appearance as queen was carefully stage managed and she was pleased with the reception she received. Both Anne and Henry kept a close eye on everyone at court to ensure that sufficient respect was shown to her. For Anne, it was the culmination of all her hopes and ambition and she adopted the motto 'the Most Happy'. In April 1533, Anne was secure in the king's continuing affection for her and she knew that she would soon be the mother of his son. Everything was exactly as she hoped.

While Anne considered herself to be 'the Most Happy' her elevation to queen was certainly not accepted by everyone. Naturally, Catherine and Mary in no way accepted Anne's marriage, as both Anne and Henry would have expected. Anne had also never been able to win the love of the people of England and, while the majority of people quietly accepted her marriage, most were privately unhappy about it. Some also actively opposed Anne and both she and Henry were determined to deal with open opposition fiercely. The state papers from 1533 are littered with examples of investigations into rudeness about Anne and her marriage and these provide something of a flavour of Anne's unpopularity. In May, for example, a merchant from Antwerp was reported to Cromwell for selling insulting images of Henry and Anne painted onto cloth. These cloth images were intended as a deliberate provocation and Spaniards and Dutchmen in the crowd 'jested and spoke opprobrious words against the king and queen'. In June, some English friars living in Antwerp were found to be publishing books against Henry's marriage to Anne. A priest was also investigated in June for calling Anne a whore and a harlot and quoting a prophecy that a queen would be burned at Smithfield. A further priest is reported to have demanded to know 'who the devil made Nan Bullen, that whore, queen?' These incidents cannot have harmed Anne personally, but they certainly angered her and cast a shadow over her happiness. The fact that both Anne and Henry considered it a problem is clear from a proclamation issued by Henry in May offering a reward for information on people speaking out against his marriage.

Although the defiance angered Anne, she had other things to concern herself with in spring 1533 and both she and Henry threw themselves into the preparations for her coronation. For Anne, it was the mark of Henry's love for her that he was prepared to crown her. Catherine of Aragon had been crowned with Henry on his accession and, for Anne, who already possessed nearly everything that her rival had once owned, the crown was the final triumph, excepting the birth of a healthy son. Henry was also determined that his son should be born to a consecrated mother and, given Anne's advancing pregnancy, it was necessary for the preparations to proceed with speed.

Anne had received almost everything that Catherine had possessed but she was still determined to show her rival just who the true queen of England was. Anne's behaviour towards Catherine and her daughter is never attractive but it is, at least, understandable. For Anne to truly be queen, Catherine had to be only princess dowager and for Anne's unborn child to be truly legitimate, Mary had to be a bastard. Anne was determined to erase any evidence of the ex-queen from court and her vindictive actions ensured that even Catherine made an unwilling contribution to her coronation. Chapuys heard a report that Henry:

> 'Had been very much grieved that the arms of the queen Catherine had been not only taken from her barge, but also rather shamefully mutilated; and that he had rather roughly rebuked the Lady's Chamberlain, not only for having taken away the said arms, but for having seized the barge, which belonged only to the queen, especially as there are in the river many others quite as suitable'.

For Anne, only Catherine's barge would truly show the world she was queen and no other barge would do. This incident caused something of a disagreement between the royal couple and Henry may have been concerned about the diplomatic troubles that Anne's actions might cause. The disagreement was not however serious and it was in Catherine's barge that Anne made her ceremonial procession to the Tower on the first day of her coronation festivities.

Anne's coronation was intended to be an extravagant display of the new order heralded by her marriage. Henry wanted to prove to the world that Anne was every inch the queen and, although it was often customary for kings to have a second coronation when they remarried, Henry intended that the celebrations would be Anne's alone. The coronation was intended to be the biggest spectacle since Henry's own coronation nearly twenty-five years before and, in order for the splendour to be fully displayed, the festivities were designed to take place over five days. Anne, at around six months pregnant, knew that she would face a gruelling series of ceremonies during the last days of May and the first days of June 1533, but she probably did not care as she considered her coronation the greatest triumph of her life and the high-point of her entire career.

On 29 May 1533, the mayor of London and representatives of all the crafts arrived by water at Greenwich, travelling in barges decked with colourful banners. Anne watched the company assemble from a window of the palace and at 3pm she made a stately appearance, walking confidently out to her barge. Once Anne was ready, the entire company set out for the Tower of London. Anne landed at Tower wharf and, as she landed, there was a great gun salute from the Tower, louder than anyone could remember. Henry came out to greet Anne 'with a noble loving countenance', before thanking the assembled company. He and Anne then retired to the royal apartments at the Tower, presumably to talk over the day's events and for Anne to rest and prepare herself for the days ahead. An enormous crowd had come out to watch Anne's procession and, while Chapuys claimed that the crowd 'showed themselves as sorry as though it had been a funeral', this was not the majority verdict and Anne herself was pleased with the numbers who had turned out to see her.

The next day was spent quietly in the Tower while Henry created 19 knights of Bath, a traditional ceremony at any coronation. Anne spent the day making the final preparations for her ceremonial entry to the city of London. On 31 May, Anne set out for Westminster in a grand procession. According to the account published by Wynkyn de Worde, first came the foreign ambassadors riding through the streets wearing blue velvet with white feathers. Next were squires, knights and most of the nobility, wearing violet clothes trimmed with ermine. Then there were the judges and the abbots. Following them rode the bishops and the favoured ambassadors of France and Venice. The lord mayor of London followed with other officials and then came Anne, sitting in a litter with a rich canopy held over her and dressed in all her finery. After her came her ladies, either following behind on their horses or riding in chariots and each displaying the wealth and finery deemed fitting for the occasion. As she left the Tower, Anne heard another gun salute and she must have been brimming with triumph as she travelled through the streets.

Anne's route through the city had been deliberately chosen as a stage to demonstrate the glory of Anne and the Tudor dynasty. At Fenchurch Street, she stopped to watch a pageant given by children before travelling on to Gracechurch where she viewed a pageant on Apollo and the nine muses. She then travelled on to Leaden Hall where, perhaps, the most elaborate of all the pageants of the day was staged. A castle with a roof designed to reach to the heavens had been erected and, as Anne watched, a white falcon, representing her own falcon emblem, descended from the sky. As the falcon landed, a child stepped forward and recited;

'Behold and see the Falcon white!
How she beginneth her wings to spread,
And for our comfort to take her flight
But where will she cease, as you do read?
A rare sight and yet to be joyed,
On the Rose, chief flower that ever was,
This bird to ' light, that all birds doth pass'.

An angel then descended from the heavens holding a crown in its hands which it placed on the falcon's head. Another child then recited:

'Honour and grace be to our Queen Anne!
For whose case an Angel celestial
Descendeth, the Falcon as white as swan,
To crown with a Diadem Imperial!
In her honour rejoice we all
For it cometh of God and not of man
Honour and grace be to our Queen Anne!'

In case anyone remained in any doubt that the falcon was meant to represent the queen, a representation of St Anne sat at the foot of the castle. Anne was thrilled at the pageants in her honour and the public rejoicing at her accession that they contained. At Cheap, Anne also passed a fountain out of which ran three types of wine. She must have been exhausted when she finally arrived at York Place where she spent the night.

Anne may well have found it difficult to sleep as she mulled over the events of the day in her head. On the whole, she would have reasoned that the day had gone well and the vast majority of the crowds do appear to have been positive, if not specifically for Anne then at least for the spectacle that had been provided. There is some indication that the day was not entirely positive and that Anne did not make quite the impression that she had hoped for. In an anonymous account, clearly exaggerated in its hostility to Anne, the author claimed that very few members of the crowd uncovered their heads and cried God save the Queen as Anne passed. This was noticed by Anne and one of her servants told the mayor to command the people to be more respectful. The mayor answered that 'he could not command people's hearts, and that even the king could not do so'. Anne's fool then called out to the crowd that 'I think you have all scurvy heads, and dare not uncover'. This still did not have the desired effect and the crowd laughed mockingly at the sight of the letters 'HA' for Henry and Anne which adorned Anne's banners. Whilst this was certainly not the behaviour of the majority of the crowd, it is clear that there were hostile observers and this may have marred the day a little for Anne.

Anne's conduct was also not without criticism and she knew that she would be compared to Catherine in her first appearances as queen. It was customary at a coronation, for the Londoners to give the king or queen a gift of money and Anne was duly provided with a purse of 2,000 nobles. According to the hostile *Chronicle of Henry VIII* instead of distributing the money amongst the captain of the guard and his men as was customary, Anne instead kept the purse for herself, stowing it in her litter beside her. Anne also complained to Henry that evening when she arrived at Westminster, saying, 'Sir, I liked the city well enough but I saw a great many caps on heads, and heard but few tongues'. It would have taken more than this to spoil Anne's day and the next morning she rose knowing that she was to be crowned queen of England.

Anne was crowned by Cranmer in Westminster Abbey and the Archbishop himself provided his own account of the coronation in his letter to Archdeacon Hawkins. According to Cranmer, the bishops and abbots assembled at the Abbey and then walked in procession to Westminster Hall where they received Anne. Anne was:

'Apparelled in a robe of purple velvet, and all the ladies and gentlemen in robes and gowns of scarlet, according to the manner used before time in such business; and so her grace sustained of each side with two bishops; the bishop of London and the bishop of Winchester, came forth in procession unto the church in Westminster, she in her hair, my lord of Suffolk bearing also before her a sceptre and a white rod, and so entered up unto the high altar, where divers ceremonies used about her, I did set the crown on her head, and then was sung Te Deum, & c. And after that was sung a solemn mass: all which while her grace sat crowned upon a scaffold, which was made between the high altar and the choir in Westminster church; which mass and ceremonies done and finished, all the assembly of noblemen brought her into Westminster Hall again, where was kept a solemn feast all that day'.

The feast that followed Anne's coronation was equally rich and Anne sat apart from the guests as she dined. The following day, Anne attended great jousts in honour of her coronation and then a second feast. Anne must have been exhausted but happy at the end of the festivities, and she knew well that her next triumph was only a few months away when she bore Henry a son.

Anne's coronation was proof of Henry's continuing love and obsession with her, and Anne felt secure in his affections. Due to Anne's advancing pregnancy, the usual summer progress was curtailed that year and Anne spent much time with her ladies. Following her coronation, Anne was the happiest she had ever been and she watched her ladies dancing in her chamber and other pastimes. Anne was also pleased to find that she was still courted by the French king and, soon after her coronation, Francis sent her a rich litter and three mules as a present. Anne also spotted an opportunity to continue her persecution of Catherine in an attempt to prove that she was the legitimate queen and she asked Henry to send to Catherine to demand a rich triumphal cloth which Catherine had brought from Spain to be used as a Christening robe. For once, Anne did not get her way and Catherine refused, responding that she would not grant such a favour 'in a case so horrible and abominable'. Anne must have been angered by Catherine's refusal but she soon had other things to worry about.

Henry had never been faithful to Catherine during their marriage and he viewed her pregnancies as an opportunity to pursue his affairs. Anne may well have thought that things would be different with her as Henry had remained faithful for nearly six years while they waited for the wedding. However, by the summer of 1533, some of Henry's affection had cooled. In August, there were rumours that he had a new mistress. By early September, Anne learned for herself that Henry had been unfaithful to her.

The name of Henry's mistress in the summer of 1533 is not known, but it was an enormous blow to Anne. Anne may well have had strong feelings for Henry herself and she knew that, until she had a son, her security was entirely dependent on Henry's passion for her. Unsurprisingly, Anne reacted angrily when she heard news of the affair and she was shocked with Henry's response. Henry responded with an attitude of righteous indignation, something that must have further infuriated the queen. According to Chapuys in a somewhat gleeful report:

'The king has taken from his treasures one of the richest and most triumphant beds which was given for the ransom of a duke of Alencon. It was as well for the Lady that it was delivered to her two months ago, for she would not have had it now; because, being full of jealousy, and not without cause, she used some words to the king at which he was displeased, and told her that she must shut her eyes, and endure as well as more worthy persons, and that she ought to know that it was in his power to humble her again in a moment more than he had exhalted her'.

Anne learned the hard way that Henry expected very different behaviour from a wife than he did from a mistress and the king refused to speak to her for two or three days after their dispute. Anne probably decided to wait until the birth of her son to raise the matter again with Henry, knowing that she would then be in an unassailable position.

Both Henry and Anne were convinced that their child would be a boy and, in order to be certain, Henry employed a number of physicians, astrologers, sorcerers and sorceresses who all confirmed that this would be the case. Anne had always been lucky and, although she would have known, in reality, that there was an even chance her child would be a girl, she probably blotted this thought from her mind. She had decided to become queen of England and she was queen. She would certainly have reasoned that she could bear the king a son. Anne eagerly awaited the birth of her child and she was full of excitement and apprehension as she took to her chamber at Greenwich on 26 August 1533 to prepare for the birth.

Henry's grandmother, the formidable Lady Margaret Beaufort, had prepared rules for the confinements of royal ladies and Anne, knowing the importance of emphasising her royal status, would have attempted to follow these. According to Margaret Beaufort, a queen should retire to her chamber about a month before the birth. The roof and walls of the chamber would be entirely hung with rich tapestries, with the exception of one window which was left unblocked to let in the light. Anne's chamber was a stuffy and uncomfortable place in late August and September 1533 and this may explain why, in fact, she did not take to her chamber until just under two weeks before the birth. Anne would have been attended only by women as she waited for the birth and as tedium set in, she must have been anxious for her pains to begin.

At 3pm on 7 September 1533, Anne's wait was over and she gave birth to a daughter. The sex of the child was a blow for both Anne and Henry and it was greeted by their 'great regret'. Henry's initial reaction was to cancel the grand tournament that he had planned to celebrate the birth of his son and Anne must have been distraught at the disappointment of her hopes. However, once the initial disappointment had subsided, both Anne and Henry accepted the birth of their daughter more happily. The baby was healthy and resembled her father and she was, at least, proof of Anne's fertility and her ability to bear a healthy child. Anne also may have sensed another way to pursue her vendetta against Catherine and there were rumours that the baby would be named Mary as a demonstration of her elder half-sister's complete irrelevance.

Although the baby was not a son, she was, as far as Henry was concerned, his heir until she was supplanted by a brother. Her birth was therefore still celebrated and Anne sent out official letters advertising that 'it hath pleased the goodness of Almighty God of his infinite mercy and grace, to send unto us at this tyme good speed in the deliverance and bringing forth of a Princess, to the great joye and inward comfort of my lord, us, and all the king's good and loving subjects'. Henry also decided to name his daughter after his mother, who had been widely considered to be heiress of England in her own time and Anne is likely to have agreed that Elizabeth was a highly suitable name. It was also, of course, coincidentally, the name of her own mother.

Elizabeth was given a grand christening as a testament to her parents' ambitions that she should be considered the only legitimate child of the king. By convention, neither Anne nor Henry attended the christening, but Anne must have felt proud as Elizabeth was carried out to her baptism. According to Hall's Chronicle, which provides a detailed account of the christening, the mayor of London and other chief citizens of the city assembled dressed in scarlet and wearing their ceremonial chains of office. The chapel had been richly decorated to mark the occasion and the citizens of London walked in procession, followed by gentlemen of the court and the king's chaplains and council. The nobility came next, dressed in their ceremonial robes. Anne's step-grandmother, the old Duchess of Norfolk, carried Elizabeth herself. Anne's uncle, Norfolk, walked beside his stepmother in the procession and Anne's father followed close behind. There was also a role for George Boleyn and he helped to hold a rich canopy above the baby, aided by other Howard relatives. Cranmer was named godfather to Elizabeth, something that must have been pleasing to Anne, with the old Duchess of Norfolk and the Marchioness of Dorset standing as godmothers. As soon as she had been baptised and named, Elizabeth was proclaimed Princess of England and heiress to England in preference to her half-sister, something that must have made Anne immensely proud.

The christening was a great success and the ceremonies ended with the return of Elizabeth to her mother's chamber. For Anne, Elizabeth's recognition as Henry's heir and the grand ceremonies that accompanied her baptism, were another triumph. Looking at her tiny daughter, Anne cannot but have wished that she had been a boy. In spite of her coronation and Henry's continuing, if cooling, love for her, Anne knew that her position was not yet entirely secure and that only the birth of a son could make her position unassailable. In September 1533 Anne knew she was capable of bearing a child and she would have expected that sons would quickly follow. She therefore threw herself into the role of queen, determined to outdo Catherine of Aragon in every respect.

CHAPTER 12

Queen Anne

Following Elizabeth's birth, Anne was able to fully establish herself as queen. She was determined to be every bit the queen that Catherine had been and, to a certain extent, she was. Late 1533 and early 1534 were still part of the high point of Anne's life and she retained Henry's support, if no longer his entire love. Despite being recognised as queen, Anne caused mixed emotions in England and on the continent and people often had a strong opinion of Anne Boleyn.

Even after her coronation and the birth of Elizabeth, Anne was deeply unpopular in England. This was due to a mixture of reasons, including the great popularity of Catherine of Aragon and Anne's comparatively lowly origins. Anne's unpopularity was also increased by suspicion surrounding her religious beliefs and, for the mostly Roman Catholic population, Anne's reformist views were guilty of leading the king astray. This was the view felt by many, but few dared express it in anything other than the sullen resentment offered at Anne's coronation. One woman, Elizabeth Barton, known as the holy maid of Kent, did dare to express such views and she was a thorn in both Anne's and Henry's sides throughout the years of the divorce and Anne's first few months as queen.

Elizabeth Barton was a young woman from Kent who suffered from a severe illness. In search of a cure for her condition, she went to church to pray for a miracle 'and when she was brought thither, and laid before the image of Our Lady, her face was wonderfully disfigured, her tongue hanging out, and her eyes being in a manner plucked out and laid upon her cheeks, and so greatly disordered. Then was there heard a voice speaking within her belly'. To the amazement of everyone present, Barton rose to her feet and declared herself cured of her illness. She quickly became a nun and word of her prophecies and visions spread widely across England. According to Thomas Cranmer, in his own account of the nun, Barton was even able to hinder Henry and Anne's marriage through her communication with both Wolsey and the previous Archbishop of Canterbury, William Warham. This in itself would never have endeared the nun to Anne, and neither Anne nor Henry would have believed Barton's prophecies which quickly turned into an attack on the king and his new wife.

Barton was not afraid to speak her mind and she declared herself a supporter of Catherine of Aragon, even attempting to meet with the ex-queen. Catherine, perceiving the potential danger in being directly associated with the nun, refused all communication with her. Catherine's great supporter John Fisher, Bishop of Rochester, and her friend, the Marchioness of Exeter met with Barton and accepted her prophecies as the divine word of God. Both Anne and Henry recognised that the nun was dangerous because she was so widely believed and she was considered by most to be 'a good, simple, and saintly woman'. Barton was afraid of no one and even secured a personal meeting with Henry where she told him that, in a short time, he 'would not only lose his kingdom, but that he should be damned, and she had seen the place and seat prepared for him in Hell'. Barton later claimed that Henry had offered to make her an abbess if she would retract her prophecies and this seems likely. Both Henry and Anne knew that it was too dangerous to act against the nun at first. When the nun claimed that Henry would cease to be king within a month of his marriage to Anne, they would have both reasoned that they would soon be able to prove her wrong.

Henry showed a restraint unusual to him over the nun but, in November 1533, well over a month after his marriage to Anne, he had Barton and her associates arrested. Both Cranmer and Cromwell had already investigated her in the summer of 1533 but, in November, Barton was subjected to a much more intense examination. In spite of her earlier defiance, she quickly confessed and, according to Cranmer, she admitted that her miraculous healing had been a sham and that 'she never had a vision in her life, but feigned them all'. This was exactly what Anne and Henry wanted to hear and Barton was publicly denounced as a fraud. A confession was not enough to save Barton and, on 20 April 1534, she and five of her associates were executed. Anne would have felt that this was a fitting punishment for a woman who had delayed her marriage and publicly denounced her queenship as sinful in the eyes of God. Anne herself would also have laughed at the credulousness displayed by Barton's supporters, having always considered Barton to be a fraud.

Anne had always been interested in religious reform and she was determined to promote it once she was queen. Even before her marriage she built a circle of men and women around her who were also interested in the new religion, among them her brother, George Boleyn. Anne never appears to have been close to her sister, but she and George were very similar characters and George rose with Anne. No portrait survives of George Boleyn but, like Anne, he was intelligent and ambitious. Even a hostile contemporary, William Cavendish, admitted that George stood out at court, writing poetically that 'God gave me [George] grace, dame Nature did hir part, Endowed me with gyfts of natural qualities'. Cavendish did go on to comment on George's lechery, something which may also account for his wife's testimony against him at his trial. George was often at court with Anne during her time as queen and he quickly gained a reputation as one of the powerful men there. In 1533, for example, George sent a servant to Flanders to buy hawks for him and managed to ensure that no dues would be payable by him on his return to Calais. George was as interested in religious reform as Anne and both sought to promote it in her household.

Although Anne is often portrayed with hostility in contemporary sources, she was not universally hated and to her fellow religious reformers, she was almost a saint. Anne's chaplain, William Latymer, wrote an account of Anne's life during the reign of her daughter and his memories of the queen were very favourable. According to Latymer, as soon as she became queen, Anne called her chaplains to her telling them that she had 'carefully chosyn you to be the lanterns and light of my courte'. She continued that:

> 'I require you, as you shall at any time herafter perceive me to decline from the right path of sownde and pure doctrine, and yelde to any maner of sensualitie, to awayte some conveniente tyme wherin you may advertise me therof; the which I promise you to accepte in very thankfull parte, addressing my selfe wholly to reformacion and yelding good example to others, for the discharge of mine awne conscience. And as to the rest of my cowrte, I straightly charge you vigilantly to wache their doinge, curiouslye to marke their proceedings, lyves and conversacions, diligently to advertise them of their dutyes, especially towarde almightie God, to instruct them the waye of virtue and grace,

to charge them to abandon and eschue all maner of vice; and above all things to embrase the wholesome doctrine and infallible knowleg of Cristes gospel, aswell in virtuous and undefiled conversacion as also in pure and syncerite understanding therof'.

Given Anne's notoriously fiery temper, it seems unlikely that any of her chaplains would have dared admonish Anne for any perceived sin. It is true that Anne wanted to preside over a household at the forefront of the religious reform and she wanted her chaplains to ensure that everyone within her household followed her lead. According to Latymer, Anne also kept a copy of the Bible in English on a desk in her apartments from which anyone was permitted to read. This was an important statement of Anne's reformist beliefs and she often read at the common desk herself as an example of how her household was expected to behave.

Although Latymer's account of Anne's religious fervour and charity is likely to be exaggerated, there is no doubt that Anne was anxious that her household should promote both the reform and godliness. Anne, along with most of her contemporaries, held very strong religious beliefs and, as queen, she saw it as her duty to set an example for her household to follow. According to Latymer, Anne frequently addressed her ladies and maids on the importance of maintaining both modesty and chastity and of not giving themselves up to idle pleasures. This is possible, although it is unlikely that Anne's household was ever as joyless as Latymer implies and there would always have been music and dancing in the queen's apartments. Anne was certainly interested in education and throughout her time as queen she would read the Bible in French as well as other French books, something which must have reminded her of her years in France. She also sought to dispel religious superstition and, during one summer progress, Anne sent commissioners to Hailes Abbey to investigate the relic of the blood of Christ held there. Anne would always have been suspicious of such a relic and, as soon as her commissioners informed her that it was either the blood of a duck or red wax, she went straight to Henry and insisted that it was removed from the Abbey. Anne also sought to promote religious reform through her charity and other good works.

Traditionally, queens were expected to be conspicuously charitable and Anne was determined to be no exception. According to the Protestant propagandist, John Foxe, Anne would send her sub-almoner to towns that she visited whilst on progress in order to obtain a list of the poor people of the parish so that her alms could be distributed efficiently. Foxe also claimed that Anne carried a purse with her at all times from which she would distribute alms 'thinking no day well spent wherein some man had not fared the better by some benefit at her hands'. Although Foxe wrote this account several years after Anne's death, his informant was Anne's cousin, Mary Howard, Duchess of Richmond, and there is likely to be some element of truth in it. Foxe's assertion that Anne gave £14,000 or £15,000 to the poor in three quarters of a year is certainly a great exaggeration as this was an enormous amount of money in Anne's time. Both Foxe and Latymer wished to show Anne in the best possible light and she was certainly not the saint they portrayed but Anne was charitable, as queens were expected to be, and particularly favoured causes close to the religious reform.

Anne was always interested in education and both she and her father and brother paid to maintain scholars at Cambridge. Anne is known to have maintained a Mr Beckynsall during his university studies on the continent, paying him £40 a year. She was not prepared to put up with any opposition to her charity and a surviving letter of Anne's to the Abbot of St Mary's shows both her charity and her queenly imperiousness that anyone should dare to go against her wishes. Anne wrote concerning a monk in the monastery, John Eldmer whom she had heard was 'of good learning, sad demeanor, and virtuous governance'. Anne continued saying that she had arranged for Eldmer to:

'Apply and continue his study and learning at my lord's university of Cambridge for the increase of virtue and learning: wherewith at that time you were well content. Yet notwithstanding the same, you, contrary to our said request (as we be credibly informed), have not only called him from his learning at the said university, but also have intricate and charged him with sundry rooms and offices in your said monastery, to the no little disturbance and inquietation of his mind, and to alienate him as much as may be from his said study and learning; to our no little marvel. We considering the good affection and desire the said dompne John Eldmer hath to the increase of virtue and learning, desire and heartily pray you, that you will permit and suffer him to repair again to the university for the intent aforesaid, giving unto him sufficient exhibition to the maintenance of his study there, or else to signify to us in writing, by this bearer, a cause reasonable why you defer to accomplish our said request made unto you in that behalf'.

Anne was determined that no one should stand in the way of her charity and, as another letter shows, even an unwilling beneficiary was no bar to Anne's purpose. In her letter to Dr Crome, Anne wrote that she was 'marvelling not a little that, albeit heretofore we have signified unto you at sundry times our pleasure concerning your promotion unto the parsonage of Aldermany, within the city of London, which we have obtained for you, yet you hitherto have deferred the taking on you of the same'. It is clear that Dr Crome was a little less eager than Anne that he should take the post offered him but this did not matter to the queen. She wanted him there and there he must go. She finished her letter stating that 'our express mind and pleasure is that you shall use no farther delays in this matter'.

Anne was determined to use her role as queen to promote religious reform and she maintained an interest in the careers of a number of scholars and churchmen with similar views to herself. According to her chaplain, William Latymer, Anne was instrumental in securing bishoprics for a number of prominent reformers, including Hugh Latimer, who became Bishop of Worcester, and, of course, Thomas Cranmer himself. Anne also supported continental reformers and, thanks to her influence, Henry's court obtained a reputation as a place of safety for continental reformers. For example, Anne heard of a reformer from France called Nicholas Bourbon who had been imprisoned for criticising the Pope. She immediately sent for him and paid his maintenance while in England. Anne also maintained a French gentlewoman, Mrs Mary, who had fled from her home due to her religion. Anne saw the traditional charity expected of a queen as a means of promoting her religious views and in this she worked closely with Thomas Cromwell. Anne would often identify those in need of patronage and then pass the practicalities of their support over to Cromwell. In May 1534, for example, Anne wrote to the minister to request that he restore Richard Herman to the English house at Antwerp after he had been expelled for promoting the Bible in English. Anne's conduct greatly increased her reputation amongst reformers and, while she was generally unpopular across England, among those who shared her religious views, 'many things might be written more of her manifold virtues, and the quiet moderation of her mild nature'. While this does not sound very recognisably Anne Boleyn, Anne's charity and promotion of religion were one aspect of her character as queen.

Anne knew that charity and religious devotion were part of the expected role of a queen, but she was aware that her primary role was to bear the king an heir. Although Elizabeth's sex was a disadvantage, Anne never resented her daughter and she was ambitious for her, for example, telling William Latymer that she wanted Elizabeth to be schooled in Hebrew, Greek, Latin, Italian, Spanish and French. Anne was preparing her to be a great princess and, perhaps, queen of France or some other nation. Both Anne and Henry were devoted to their precocious and healthy daughter and, according to the *Chronicle of Henry VIII:*

> 'They were very particular in rearing her, and when she was two years old she talked and walked like any other child of four. It was God's will that Anne should have no other children, and day and night she would not let this daughter of hers out of her sight. Whenever the queen came out in the royal palace where the canopy was, she had a cushion placed underneath for her child to sit upon'.

While it is an exaggeration to suggest that Anne would not let Elizabeth out of her sight, she was certainly devoted to her daughter and it must have been a great wrench for her when, in December 1533, Elizabeth was given her own household as befitted the Princess of England. In spite of her misgivings about parting from Elizabeth, Anne was always careful to guard her daughter's position and she closely supervised the preparations for Elizabeth's household and her journey out of London. Anne would have felt proud as she saw her daughter off in a great procession headed by Norfolk and much of the rest of the nobility. Elizabeth's journey became something of a triumphal progress and, according to Chapuys, 'although there was a shorter and better road, yet for greater solemnity, and to insinuate to the people that she is the true Princess, she was taken through this town'.

To Anne, the court must suddenly have seemed empty without Elizabeth but she was able to visit her daughter regularly and both Henry and Anne delighted in playing with their daughter and showing her off to the world. In April 1534, for example, they visited Elizabeth at Eltham and both were pleased with the fair-haired princess's progress. Elizabeth resembled Anne facially but she had Henry's colouring and, according to Sir William Kingston, one of the gentlemen present at Eltham, Elizabeth was 'a godely child as hath been seen, and her Grace is much in the King's favour as a godely child should be'. Both Anne and Henry had every reason to be delighted with their pretty daughter in April 1534 for, only the month before, she had officially been declared heiress of England by parliament.

Henry and Anne had always determined that their marriage should be the king's legitimate marriage and that his marriage to Catherine had always been invalid. This meant that Mary, as the king's daughter by a woman who was never his wife, could never be heiress of England. While this made perfect sense to both Henry and Anne, this was not the view held by much of England and most people saw Mary as the true heiress. Although Henry had Elizabeth proclaimed Princess of England at her baptism both he and Anne wanted to further safeguard their child's position and, in March 1534 parliament passed the first Act of Succession, setting out that:

> 'The said Lady Katherine shall be from henceforth called and reputed only dowager to Prince Arthur and not queen of this realm. And that the lawful matrimony had and solemnised between your Highness and your most dear and entirely beloved wife queen Anne shall be established, and taken for undoubtful, true, sincere, and perfect ever hereafter'.

Anne followed the progress of the Act closely and its terms finally enshrined her position in law. Under the terms of the Act, Henry's heirs were to be sons born to him by Anne. In the absence of such sons, his next heirs were sons born to a later wife. Finally, in the absence of any sons, Henry's heirs were to be his daughters by Anne, a tacit acknowledgment that Henry did not, as yet, actually have a son. The Act also made it high treason for a person 'by writing, print, deed, or act procure to do, or cause to be procured or done, anything or things to the prejudice, slander, disturbance, or derogation of the said lawful matrimony solemnised between your majesty and the said Queen Anne'. This was everything that Anne had hoped for and Henry also caused parliament to pass an Act requiring everyone in England to swear an oath to be obedient to Henry and to his heirs by Anne.

, Henry and Anne were determined to ensure that their marriage was recognised as lawful by everyone in the kingdom and during the parliament in March 1534, Henry ordered every lord, knight and burgess to swear the oath of succession. He also sent commissioners around the kingdom to take the oath in every parish. This was an unprecedented step for the king to take and, for the most part, measures taken to ensure that people swore were successful. According to the Chronicler, Wriothesley, for example, on the same day that the Holy Maid of Kent was executed:

'All the craftes in London were called to their halls, and there were sworne on a booke to be true to Queene Anne and to believe and take her for lawfull wife of the Kinge and rightfull Queene of Englande, and utterlie to thincke the Ladie Marie, daughter of the Kinge by Queene Katherin, but as a bastarde, and thus to doe without any scrupulosity of conscience; also all the curates and prestes in London and thoroweout Englande were also sworne before the lorde of Canterburie and other Bishopps; and allso all countries in Englande were sworne in likewise, everie man in the shires and townes were they dwelled'.

While everyone was required to swear, not everyone did. Catherine and Mary, as expected by both Anne and Henry, refused. More worryingly for the couple, the influential John Fisher, Bishop of Rochester, and Henry's ex-chancellor, Thomas More, also refused to swear. For Anne, a refusal to swear was a direct challenge to the legitimacy of both her marriage and her child and all those who refused the oath quickly became her enemies. In April 1534 Anne would have reasoned that she was in a far stronger position than any of her enemies and she would have known by then that she would shortly bear a child and, hopefully, Henry's longed-for son. In April 1534 Anne cannot have foreseen the dark clouds gathering on the horizon ahead of her.

CHAPTER 13

Rebels and Traitoresses

For Anne, 1534 began well and she must have felt secure in her position as queen. However, she would also have been aware that, with both Catherine and Mary still maintaining their opposition, she could never be completely secure. Henry's infidelity in the summer of 1533 must also have played on her mind and, while she still retained his support and affection, she certainly realised that his fervour towards her had abated in the first year of their marriage. Anne knew that in order to safeguard her position she needed a son and, as time moved on, troubles slowly began to mount up for her. By summer 1534, the honeymoon of Anne's marriage and queenship was over.

Anne always expected opposition to her queenship from Catherine of Aragon and it would have come as no surprise when the older woman maintained her resistance following her demotion to Princess Dowager. Catherine was a woman as determined as Anne and the two women loathed each other. It is hard to excuse Anne concerning the campaign of vindictiveness that she waged against both Catherine and her daughter and she certainly contributed to making their lives miserable. Anne did at least act for her own self-preservation and to ensure the position of her daughter. This does not excuse her, but it does explain her actions. Henry, on the other hand, acted with calculated cruelty towards his ex-wife and eldest daughter and he was determined to crush their opposition. People simply did not defy Henry VIII and Henry displayed a ruthlessness towards the two women that he would later show towards Anne and her own daughter. Even Anne may have seen his conduct as the warning it was and it would only have made her more determined to ensure that her own position was secure, at the expense of Catherine and Mary.

Anne and Henry attacked Catherine soon after the annulment of her marriage was pronounced. While neither Anne nor Henry can have expected Catherine to acknowledge their marriage, they may have hoped that under enough pressure she would at least become less openly defiant. The first attempt to break Catherine's position was made in July 1533, when Lord Mountjoy was sent to Catherine to inform her of her new title of Princess Dowager. According to Lord Mountjoy, they:

'Found her lying on a pallet, as she had pricked her foot with a pin, and could not stand, and was also sore annoyed with a cough. On our declaring that our instructions were to her as Princess Dowager, she took exception to the name, persisting that she was the king's true wife, and her children were legitimate, which she would claim to be true during her life. To our assertion that the marriage with Anne Boleyn had been adjudged lawful by the universities, the lords and commons, she said the king might do in his realm by his royal power what he would; that the cause was not theirs but the Pope's to judge, as she had already answered the duke of Norfolk. To other arguments, that she might damage her daughter and servants, she replied she would not damn her own soul on any consideration, or from any promises the king might make her'.

Lord Mountjoy cannot have relished his commission to visit Catherine and, to his horror, when she was shown a copy of his orders, she scored through the words 'Princess Dowager' violently and replaced them with 'Queen'. Catherine's defiance infuriated Anne and Henry, but it cannot have been unexpected and they continued, throughout 1534 and 1535, to try to break Catherine's will.

Henry and Anne were determined to keep Catherine in exile away from London and, soon after the return of Lord Mountjoy to court, Catherine was ordered to move to a house further from London. According to Chapuys, the move did not go according to Henry's plan and, as Catherine travelled, crowds assembled to see her. They showed her great affection and ran after her litter calling her queen in defiance of the king. This was exactly what Anne and Henry did not want to hear and it only hardened their resolve towards Catherine and her daughter. In December 1533, they resolved to move Catherine again, this time to Somersham, a house surrounded by both a moat and marshes and, as Catherine had heard , 'the most unhealthy house in England'. Catherine absolutely refused to go, even when the Duke of Suffolk arrived and dismissed the bulk of her household. When it became apparent that Suffolk had instructions to remove her by force, Catherine locked herself in her chamber and declared through a hole in the wall that the Duke would have to break down the door. Suffolk was forced to return to court leaving Catherine where she was. Once again, Anne and Henry were furious at Catherine's refusal to admit the fact of their marriage and, in exasperation, they turned their attention to her daughter.

Mary, who only turned eighteen in February 1534, must have seemed a much easier target to Anne. Throughout the years of the divorce, Mary had consistently supported her mother and Anne may have underestimated the strength of Mary and Catherine's commitment to each other. The pair had not been permitted to meet since the summer of 1531 when Henry left Catherine, but they still found ways to communicate in secret. In September 1533, Catherine heard rumours that Mary was to become a target of the king's anger and wrote to her daughter to fortify her for the struggle ahead. Catherine wrote:

> 'Daughter, I heard such tidings today that I do perceive, if it be true, the time is come that Almighty God will prove you; and I am very glad of it, for I trust he doth handle you with a good love. I beseech you to agree to His pleasure with a merry heart; and be you sure that, without fail, he will not suffer you to perish if you beware to offend him'.

Catherine ended her letter telling Mary to obey Henry in everything, save only where she would offend God. Anne and Henry can have had no idea of just how hardened Mary's resolve was. Henry always saw Mary as a disobedient child who needed to be brought to heel, but for Anne, following the birth of Elizabeth, it was more personal and Mary was every bit her daughter's rival as Catherine was hers.

Henry's attacks on Mary began soon after Elizabeth's birth and, by 15 September 1533, her household servants had been ordered to remove her livery and replace it with that of the king. This was, essentially, a public announcement of Mary's 'illegitimacy', and only Elizabeth, as the king's legitimate daughter, was to be given her own household. Henry also sent a deputation of his council to order Mary to relinquish her claim to be Princess of England. The council members must have thought that Mary would be a more malleable target than her mother but, in this, they would be sadly disappointed. Mary greeted them imperiously and:

'Without taking the advice of anybody, as no communication would have been permitted her, replied to the Commissioners, and likewise wrote to the King, that she would be as obedient to his commands as any slave, but she had no right to renounce or derogate from the titles and prerogatives that God, nature, and her parents had given her; that being daughter of the king and queen, she had a right to be styled Princess; and that her father might do with her as he pleased, she would do nothing expressly or tacitly in prejudice of her legitimacy, nor of the cause of her mother'.

Chapuys concluded that this treatment was due to Anne's 'importunity and malignity' but, while Anne would have been well aware of, and approving of, the treatment meted out to Mary, it was Henry who was directly behind the attack on his eldest daughter. Anne would not have had the power to act in this way alone.

Mary's anger infuriated both Henry and Anne and in early November 1533, Henry announced that Mary's household would be broken up and that she would be sent to serve Elizabeth as one of her ladies. This was the ultimate humiliation for Mary, but she still would not be cowed and she moved to join Elizabeth in December. Anne would have been angered to hear that Mary still protested loudly and, upon arrival in Elizabeth's household, Mary refused to go and pay her respects to the 'Princess', replying that 'she knew no other Princess in England except herself and that the daughter of Madame de Penebrok had no such title'. Mary added, maddeningly for Anne, that, since her father acknowledged Elizabeth to be his daughter, she would call her sister, in the same way that she called Henry's bastard son, Richmond, brother.

Such comments not only enraged Anne, but she also saw them as a direct challenge to her beloved daughter. Anne knew well that there was no one in England more dangerous to Elizabeth than Mary and she was constantly afraid that Henry's heart would soften towards his eldest daughter. Anne was given direct control over Mary by the king and appointed her aunt, Lady Shelton, as Mary's governess. This meant that Anne received direct information from Mary's household and she was able to monitor Mary accordingly. She was determined that Henry and Mary should not meet and, in January 1534, when Henry visited Elizabeth without Anne, Anne obtained his promise that he would not see his eldest daughter and Mary was kept in her room. Anne was alarmed to hear that, as the king mounted his horse to leave, he looked up to the roof of the house and saw Mary kneeling on a terrace, looking towards her father. Instinctively, Henry put his hand to his hat to salute Mary and was eagerly followed by those accompanying him. Upon Henry's return to court, Anne berated him for this, complaining that he did not keep Mary closely confined enough. She also reconsidered her earlier plans to have Mary brought to court and made to carry her train, for fear that the king's affection for Mary should be reawakened.

Anne's treatment of Mary stemmed from fear for her daughter, as her treatment of Catherine was due to fear for herself. In the early years of her marriage, Anne was determined to bring Mary to heel and, once it became clear that the humiliation of being moved to Elizabeth's household had not worked, Anne tried to befriend Mary instead. In March 1534, during a visit to Elizabeth, Anne sent a message to Mary, asking her to visit her and offering to be the means of reconciliation between Mary and her father, assuring her that she would be as well or even better treated than she ever had been before. The price for Mary of Anne's offer was an acknowledgment that she was illegitimate and that her parents had never been married, something that she would eventually acknowledge, but not during Anne's lifetime. Mary replied saying that there was no queen in England except her mother, but that she would be grateful if the king's mistress would intercede with him for her. Anne was furious at the response and, after threatening Mary, ranted that she 'intended to bring down the pride of this unbridled Spanish blood'.

That Anne would have been kind towards her stepdaughter if Mary would only acknowledge her illegitimacy is clear from another incident recorded in the *Life of Jane Dormer*, who was a friend of Mary's. According to Jane Dormer, Anne and Mary once found themselves attending mass together at Eltham whilst Anne was visiting her daughter. At the end of the service, Mary made a low curtsey. When Anne returned to her rooms, one of her ladies told her excitedly that Mary had made reverence to her as they left the chapel. This was what Anne had always hoped for and she replied that 'if we had seen it, we would have done as much to her'. Anne then sent a message of friendship to Mary, saying:

'The queen salutes your grace with much affection and craves pardon, understanding that at your parting from the oratory, you made a courtesy to her, which if she had seen, she would have answered you with the like, and she desires that this may be an entrance of friendly correspondence, which your grace shall find completely to be embraced on her part'.

Upon receiving the message, Mary answered that the queen, her mother, could not have sent her this message as she was not present in the house. Mary then stated that her reverence had been made to the altar and certainly not to Lady Anne Boleyn. Anne railed against her stepdaughter when she heard this, as she often did when she received word of Mary's defiance.

Catherine and Mary's great supporter, Chapuys, believed that Anne was trying to kill both Catherine and Mary. He heard a rumour that Anne had paid someone to claim that they had had a revelation from God that she would not conceive a son whilst the two women lived and that Catherine and Mary were 'rebels and traitresses deserving death'. According to Chapuys' report on 11 February 1534 he had heard a rumour that Anne had told the Earl of Northumberland (her former suitor, Henry Percy), that she was determined to poison Mary. In June of that same year he also heard that:

> 'The king's concubine has said more than once, and with great assurance, that when the king has crossed the sea, and she remains gouvernante, as she will be, she will use her authority to put the said Princess to death, either by hunger or otherwise. On Rochford, her brother, telling her this would anger the king, she said she did not care even if she were burned alive for it after'.

This seems more to be evidence of the fiery Anne's inability to control her temper than any deliberate plot to murder Mary and there is no evidence that she ever sought to actually kill Henry's daughter and his ex-wife. Anne may have wished them dead, but that is a very different proposition from actually attempting murder. Also, the simple fact is that Mary survived Anne, and Catherine lived until 1536. If Anne had wanted to poison either woman, it would have been a simple matter to do so. They were annoyances and she hated them, but Anne was no murderess.

Catherine and Mary were not the only members of Anne's extended family who caused her irritation during 1534 and, in the summer of that year, Anne's sister, Mary Boleyn, appeared at court visibly pregnant and announced that she had secretly married one of her servants, the lowly William Stafford. Anne felt that she had been elevated to the head of the Boleyn family by her marriage and was furious that her sister had thrown herself away so cheaply and without consulting her. Anne immediately ordered that her sister should be banished from the court, cutting Mary off from all financial support. Anne and Mary Boleyn were never close but Mary was shocked by her sister's reaction. Finding herself destitute, she wrote to Cromwell, asking him to intercede with her sister for her:

'And good master secretary, sue for us to the king's highness, and beseech his highness that it will please him of his goodness to speak to the queen's grace for us, for I perceive her grace is so highly displeased with us both, that, without the king to be so good lord to us as to sue for us, we are never like to recover her grace's favour, which is too heavy to bear. For God's sake help us, for we have now been married a quarter of a year, I thank God, and too late now to recall that again. But if I were at my liberty and I might choose, I assure you, master secretary, I had rather beg my bread with him than be the greatest queen christened.

And I beseech you, good master secretary, pray my lord and father and my lady to be good to us, and let us have their blessings, and my husband their good-will. Also, I pray my lord Norfolk and my brother to be good to us. I dare not write to them, they are so cruel against me'.

Anne was furious that Mary, a Boleyn, should have so little ambition. Anne may also have been angered by Mary's defiance in her letter and by her assertion that she would rather beg for a living than change places with her sister. In the summer of 1534 Mary's pregnancy may also have been offensive to her sister and it was around this time that Anne lost her own second child.

Anne would have known as soon as Elizabeth was born that she was expected to quickly conceive another child and, by December 1533, she would have begun to suspect that she was pregnant. Both Anne and Henry must have been ecstatic and Anne confidently expected that it would be a boy this time. Anne's pregnancy progressed well and, by April 1534, she was visibly pregnant. As with her first pregnancy, Anne could not resist flaunting her expanding figure and she knew that it was a constant reproach to Catherine. By July, Anne would have been expecting the birth of her child imminently and when it was suggested that Henry should cross to France to meet with the French king, Anne sent her brother to France to request that the meeting should be postponed until after the birth so that she could attend.

Anne was not to bear her longed for son in the summer of 1534 and, at some point, she miscarried or gave birth to a stillborn child. Sources are silent on the fate of Anne's second pregnancy and it was probably a girl. Anne was devastated and Henry angry that she had once again failed to produce a son and this time there was not even a living daughter as compensation. To make matters worse for Anne, when she emerged from her sick bed, she was confronted with the news that Henry had once again taken a mistress. By late September there were rumours that Henry had fallen in love with another lady and Anne angrily confronted the king as she had done before. Henry reacted furiously, telling Anne that 'she had good reason to be content with what he had done for her, which he would not do now if the thing were to begin and that she should consider from what she had come'.

Anne was horrified with Henry's comments and she recognised them as a reference to the insecurity of her position. Without a son, Anne was as vulnerable as Catherine of Aragon had been and her security entirely depended on the lessening love of the king. Anne decided to take action against Henry's new mistress to ensure that she did not remain her rival and she conspired with her sister-in-law, Lady Rochford, to attempt to have Henry's mistress banished from the court. No details of this conspiracy survive but it probably involved Lady Rochford making some complaint against the mistress or picking a quarrel with her. Regardless of how their plan worked, it failed, and Anne was horrified to find that it was Lady Rochford who was banished from the court and not her husband's mistress.

Henry's affair with his mistress continued for the rest of 1534 and Anne must have felt desperate as she watched her influence over the king begin to slip away. Henry had always been faithful to Anne before their marriage, but he certainly had no intention of remaining faithful afterwards. Anne found it impossible to simply sit back and pretend not to notice his affairs as Catherine had done before her. Anne spent the last months of 1534 and the first half of 1535 in a near hysterical state of anxiety as Henry strayed from her and month after month she found that she had failed to conceive. In January 1535, Anne gave a clear demonstration of the stress she was under when, while sitting with the French ambassador at a banquet, she suddenly burst out laughing. The ambassador:

'Was much annoyed, and knitting his eyebrows, said "How is that madam; are you mocking me?" Upon which, the lady, after somewhat restraining her laughter, made her excuses, saying "I could not help laughing at the king's proposition of introducing your secretary to me, for whilst he was looking out for him he happened to meet a lady, who was the cause of his forgetting everything"'.

Anne was always subject to fits of laughter when she came under stress and she must have felt that Henry was slipping from her grasp.

As Anne's star began to wane, her stepdaughter, Mary's, rose and members of Henry's court began to pay secret visits to her when they should have been paying their respects to Elizabeth. It was also telling that, when Elizabeth's establishment moved to another house, Mary was provided with a litter of velvet which matched that of her younger half-sister. Previously, Mary's lower status had been signified by the provision of a litter of leather. Anne also found that her supporters began to drift away from her and, in late 1534, she finally broke completely with the Duke of Norfolk, unleashing her anger and stress on her uncle. While Norfolk might once have been prepared to take abuse from his fiery niece, he would no longer stand for it, calling Anne a great whore as he left the room.

By spring 1535, Anne was alone at court and vulnerable. Many people around her had been alienated by her temper and others were paying court to her stepdaughter or to the king's mistress. Anne's influence over Henry was also almost non-existent, but she was still able to cling on to the knowledge that, although he was not faithful to her and his obsession had gone, she was his wife and he was as publicly committed to their marriage as he had always been. Anne knew that she had to win Henry back and that she had to conceive a son and, as her enemy Chapuys pointed out, this was entirely possible. Anne, like no other, 'knows well how to manage him'.

CHAPTER 14

No More Boys By Her

Anne began 1535 in a weakened position. Her miscarriage in the summer of 1534 had been a blow and her failure to conceive again must have been a grave concern. Henry had risked a great deal for his marriage to Anne and both knew that it could not be thrown away lightly, whatever Henry's personal feelings towards his wife. Anne knew just how dependent she was on Henry and she worked hard to ensure that she remained the most important woman in his life, even if she also had to accept that he had mistresses. By the summer of 1535 there had been a reconciliation between the couple, helped in no small part by a demonstration by Henry of his belief in their marriage in June and July 1535.

John Fisher, Bishop of Rochester and Sir Thomas More had been sent to the Tower for their refusal to take the oath of succession back in 1534. With the exception of Catherine and Mary, Fisher and More were the most high profile people in England to refuse the oath and, as a result, Henry attempted to convince them, first through reasoning and then through increasingly harsh imprisonment. Fisher had always been a great supporter of Catherine and neither Henry nor Anne can have thought it likely that the old man would change his opinions. They may however have hoped that More would be more malleable and it is clear that, unlike Fisher, he did not actively oppose Anne's marriage, writing to Cromwell that 'so am I he that among others his Grace's faithful subjects, his Highness being in possession of his marriage and this noble woman really anointed queen, neither murmur at it nor dispute upon it, nor never did nor will'. More's quarrel was never with Anne nor her marriage, but his scruples about taking the oath recognising the king as the head of the Church amounted to the same thing for both Anne and Henry.

Fisher was tried for treason at Westminster on 17 June 1535 and sentenced to death. Both Anne and Henry must have felt the sentence was vindicated when word reached them that Fisher had been made a cardinal by the new Pope, Paul III, and that his cardinal's hat was on its way to England. On hearing the news, Henry commented dryly 'well, let the Pope send him a hatt when he will, but I will so provide that when soever it commeth he shall weare it on his shoulders for head shall he have none to sett it on'. For Anne, Fisher had always been her enemy and she was unconcerned when he was executed on Tower Hill on 22 June 1535 and his head set on London Bridge. More followed Fisher to the scaffold on 6 July 1535. The executions of Fisher and More were, for Anne, a public statement by Henry of his commitment to their marriage and the royal supremacy over the Church that the marriage had ushered in. Even if Henry loved Anne less in summer 1535, Anne knew that he was still committed to her and he would remain so, if only she could bear him a son.

Anne and Henry became reconciled with each other in the summer of 1535 after a difficult year following Anne's second pregnancy. Anne had come to accept Henry's infidelities as a certainty, even if she could never fully ignore them as Catherine had done. For Henry, the deaths of Fisher and More and the public statement of commitment to his marriage that they made may also have reawakened his interest in Anne. At the very least, Henry still desperately needed a legitimate son and Anne, as his wife, was the only person who could provide him with this. Both Anne and Henry would have suspected that this might take some time and, according to accounts of Anne's trial, for all Henry's eye for women, he was often incapable of performing the sexual act with his wife. In spite of this, both Anne and Henry went off on their summer and autumn progress in good spirits, hopeful for the future.

The royal court in the sixteenth century was always itinerant and Anne was well used to a life of constant travel from her years at Henry's court. The mobility of the court served a dual purpose, allowing Henry's subjects to see their monarch personally and in order to allow recently vacated palaces to be thoroughly cleaned. The summer progress of 1535 took Anne and Henry out in a westerly direction from London. In October they visited Salisbury and Portchester and by November they had reached Windsor. Earlier, in September, they also paid a visit to Wolf Hall in Wiltshire, the family home of Jane Seymour, one of Anne's maids. Anne may, perhaps, have noticed an attraction between Henry and Jane but she would have tried to put it out of her mind. In any event, Anne would have hoped that she would not have to worry about the security of her position as queen for much longer and by the time the court returned to London in late 1535 she was pregnant for the third time.

For Anne, even better news arrived at court just after Christmas when word was delivered that Catherine of Aragon was ill and not expected to live. From Anne's point of view, Catherine's very existence had blighted nearly ten years of her life and she was joyous when she heard the news. Henry was also glad to hear of his ex-wife's illness and happily gave Chapuys permission to visit Catherine, reasoning that she could no longer cause him any difficulties. Chapuys set out at once, riding with haste to Kimbolton where Catherine was staying.

Chapuys found Catherine in bed where she had spent several days. She was glad to see the ambassador and according to his report:

'After I had kissed hands she took occasion to thank me for the numerous services I had done her hitherto and the trouble I had taken to come and see her, a thing that she had very ardently desired, thinking that my coming would be salutary for her, and at all events, if it pleased God to take her, it could be a consolation to her to die under my guidance and not unprepared, like a beast. I gave her every hope, both of her health and otherwise, informing her of the offers the king had made to me of what houses she would, and to cause her to be paid the remainder of certain arrears, adding, for her further consolation, that the king was very sorry for her illness, and on this I begged her to take heart and get well, if for no other consideration, because the union and peace of Christendom depended upon her life'.

Chapuys stayed with Catherine for four days and she gradually began to improve with his company, managing to sleep more easily and to take a little food. Catherine told Chapuys to return to court so that Henry could not say that he had abused his licence to visit her. He therefore returned to court, hopeful of the ex-queen's survival. On his arrival back at court on 7 January, Cromwell sent for him to inform him that Catherine had died.

Although Chapuys was not present at Catherine's death, he soon received an account of it and was pleased to see that she had died in as saintly a manner as he believed she had lived. For two days after Chapuys left, Catherine had seemed better but by the early hours of 7 January it was clear to everyone that she was dying. As she felt death approaching, Catherine begged those standing by to pray for her soul and for God to pardon the king. She also called for paper and composed her last letter to Henry, showing that, in spite of everything, she still retained her affection for him:

'My most dear lord, king and husband,
The hour of my death now drawing on, the tender love I owe you forceth me, my case being such, to commend myself to you, and to put you in remembrance with a few words of the health and safeguard of your soul which you ought to prefer before all worldly matters, and before the care and pampering of your body, for the which you have cast me into many calamities and yourself into many troubles. For my part, I pardon you everything, and I wish to devoutly pray God that He will pardon you also. For the rest, I commend unto you our daughter Mary, beseeching you to be a good father unto her, as I have heretofore desired. I entreat you also, on behalf of my maids, to give them marriage portions, which is not much, they being but three. For all my other servants I solicit the wages due them, and a year more, lest they be unprovided for. Lastly, I make this vow, that mine eyes desire you above all things'.

Catherine's letter is testament to the enduring love she felt for Henry, in spite of the years of cruelty she had endured. She died shortly after it was written.

Catherine's letter was dispatched to Henry's court with news of her death. According to the report of the Catholic propagandist, Sander, Henry could not stop himself from weeping when he read the letter. This is very far from the truth and, in reality, both Henry and Anne greeted the news as though a great weight had been lifted from their shoulders. For Henry, Catherine's continued existence had meant the prospect of war with her powerful nephew and, for Anne, there was always the fear that Henry would be forced to return to his first wife. On 7 January 1536, Anne finally felt secure. Catherine of Aragon was dead and the son that Anne dearly hoped she was carrying would be born into a world where only Anne could claim to be Henry's wife. Both Henry and Anne were overjoyed with the news and they celebrated Catherine's death by wearing yellow. According to Chapuys, when he heard the news, Henry:

'exclaimed "God be praised that we are free from all suspicion of war"; and that the time had come that he would manage the French better than he had done hitherto, because they would do now whatever he wanted from a fear lest he should ally himself again with your Majesty [Charles V], seeing that the cause which disturbed your friendship was gone. On the following day, Sunday, the king was clad all over in yellow, from top to toe, except the white feather he had in his bonnet, and the Little Bastard [Elizabeth] was conducted to mass with trumpets and other great triumphs. After dinner the king entered the room in which the ladies danced, and there did several things like one transported with joy. At last, he sent for his Little Bastard, and carrying her in his arms he showed her first to one and then to another. He has done the like on other days since, and has run some courses at Greenwich'.

Anne and all her supporters were equally overjoyed and Thomas Boleyn exclaimed that it was a pity that Mary did not keep company with her mother. Anne also caused outrage by claiming that she was sorry about Catherine's death 'not indeed because she is dead, but because her death has been so honourable'. Anne had always been outspoken and she never cared who heard her speak. To observers her words were shocking and it was unsurprising that rumours quickly circulated concerning Anne's role in Catherine's death.

As soon as he heard the news of Catherine's illness Chapuys was suspicious that poison could have been involved. While he was still at Kimbolton he questioned Catherine's physician and was concerned to hear that Catherine had become worse after she drank some Welsh beer. As was usual, soon after her death, Catherine's body was opened up and examined in a bid to determine what had killed her. Catherine's organs were all found to be healthy with the exception of her heart 'which was quite black and hideous, and even after he had washed it three times it did not change colour. He divided it through the middle and found the interior the same colour, which also would not change on being washed, and also some black round thing which clung closely to the outside of the heart'. For Chapuys and many other people in England, this was clear evidence that Catherine had been murdered and for them, there was only one suspect: Anne. Although there is no doubt that Anne hated Catherine, it is very unlikely that she murdered her. By 1536, Catherine was fifty, elderly for the time, and she had spent several years in difficulties. If Anne had wanted to murder Catherine, she would have done it long before 1536. Certainly, Anne saw Catherine's death as beneficial, but she did not murder her. She only had to wait for nature to take its course.

With Catherine dead, Anne decided that she would make one final attempt at befriending Mary. Within days of Catherine's death, Anne had written to her stepdaughter, saying that 'if she would lay aside her obstinacy and obey her father, she would be the best friend to her in the world and be like another mother, and would obtain for her anything she could ask, and that if she wished to come to court she would be exempted from holding the tail of her gown'. Anne must have felt that this was a very generous offer. With Catherine gone, Mary no longer had the divided loyalties that she had felt towards her parents and Anne, secure in the knowledge of her pregnancy felt that, perhaps, Mary would finally come to understand that it was Anne who had won, not Catherine. Mary however refused point-blank to have any dealings with Anne, sending Anne into a rage. This was the last attempt that Anne would make to befriend her stepdaughter and she wrote a letter to her aunt, Lady Shelton, who was Mary's governess, venting her true feelings towards Catherine's daughter:

'Mrs Shelton, my pleasure is that you do not further move the Lady Mary to be towards the King's Grace otherwise than it pleases herself. What I have done has been more for charity than for anything the king or I care what road she takes, or whether she will change her purpose, for if I have a son, as I hope shortly, I know what will happen to her; and therefore, considering the word of God, to do good to one's enemy, I wished to warn her beforehand, because I have daily experience that the king's wisdom is such as not to esteem her repentance of her rudeness and unnatural obstinacy when she has no choice. By the law of God and of the king, she ought clearly to acknowledge her error and evil conscience if her blind affection had not so blinded her eyes that she will see nothing but what pleases herself. Mrs Shelton, I beg you not to think to do me any pleasure by turning her from any of her wilful courses, because she could not do me [good] or evil; and do your duty according to the king's command, as I am assured you do'.

While this letter was addressed to Lady Shelton, it was meant for Mary and contained a warning to the princess. While Anne had no son, Mary was a threat to Elizabeth and Anne could not tolerate her. But, if Anne bore Henry a son, Mary's existence would be a threat to the king's longed for heir and Mary could then expect to feel her father's full wrath for her refusal to conform to his will.

In spite of his harsh treatment of Catherine in the last years of her life, as far as Henry was concerned, Catherine was still a princess of Spain and the widow of his elder brother. He decided to give her a grand funeral to mark her status as Princess Dowager of Wales. This would be very far from what Catherine herself had wanted but, for Anne, it was once again a mark of Henry's continuing commitment to their marriage. Catherine was to be buried as 'the right excellent and noble Princesse the Lady Catherin, Doughter to the right highe and mighty Prince Ferdinand, late king of Castle, and late wife to the noble and excellent prince Arthur, brother to our sovereign lorde Kinge Henry the viiith'. Anne would have been pleased that Catherine had finally been completely denied the title of queen but she would have had little chance to savour the details of the ceremony. On the very day of Catherine's funeral, Anne went into premature labour after only around three and a half months of pregnancy, miscarrying a male foetus.

For Anne, the loss of her son was a disaster and she wept bitterly as she lay in her chamber. Henry was also grief-stricken and this quickly turned to anger against the woman that he had once loved above all else. As soon as he heard the news, Henry stormed into Anne's chamber to confront her angrily and 'bewailing and complaining unto her the loss of his boy'. Anne, for once, was entirely lost for words and made no response to the king. Henry then struck terror into her heart, saying that he could see that 'he would have no more boys by her' before muttering that he would speak to her again when she had recovered. Anne must have felt as though her world had collapsed as her husband stormed out the room. As she lay in her sickbed, Anne heard the rumours flying around court and she was horrified to hear that Henry was claiming that 'he had made this marriage, seduced by witchcraft, and for this reason he considered it null; and that this was evident because God did not permit them to have any male issue and that he believed that he might take another wife, which he gave to understand that he had some wish to do'.

While she recovered, Anne continually wept for fear that the king would discard her as he had discarded Catherine. While she remained in her chamber she prepared her arguments to explain why the miscarriage was not her fault and, as soon as she was well enough, she went straight to the king. According to a number of sources, Anne attributed the loss of her son to two principal causes. On 24 January, only a few days before the disaster, Henry had fallen heavily from his horse and was knocked unconscious. At the time, there was some fear of his life and the Duke of Norfolk was sent to inform Anne of the calamity. The possibility that Henry might die would have terrified her. Even if, as is likely, any love she had felt for him was rapidly evaporating, she still knew that he was her protector and the only bar between her and the hostile crowds. If Henry had died, Anne, who was named regent and governor of her children in the event of Henry's early death, would have had to attempt to secure the crown for Elizabeth or her unborn son. Anne knew as well as anyone the powerful support Mary could muster and she knew that Henry's death would lead to civil war and, very possibly, a foreign invasion.

It is very easy to imagine Anne's terror when word was brought to her of the king's fall and, according to Chapuys, Anne saw this as one of the principal causes of her miscarriage and 'she wished to lay the blame on the duke of Norfolk, whom she hates, saying he frightened her by bringing the news of the fall the king had six days before. But it is well known that this is not the cause, for it was told her in a way that she should not be alarmed or attach much importance to it'. Henry dismissed this argument and it is clear that Anne was clutching at straws. Her second argument does appear to have struck home with Henry. According to George Wyatt, as usual, Henry saw Anne's pregnancy as an opportunity for him to conduct an extra-marital affair. Anne would have known by then that she was expected to make no comment on this and, while she was still hoping for the birth of a son she obeyed, presumably hoping to be able to remonstrate with Henry later when a prince made her position secure. In the days before her miscarriage Anne, who had tried her best to turn a blind eye, entered a room to find Henry caressing Jane Seymour as she sat on his knee. This was too much for Anne and, as she remonstrated with Henry following her miscarriage she claimed 'that the love she bore him was far greater than that of the late queen, so that her heart broke when she saw he loved others' and she lost her child.

For once, Henry was lost for words and, for a few days at least, did feel remorse, leaving Jane Seymour behind at Greenwich the next time the court moved. For Anne, it was an empty victory. She was still without a son and, with the death of Catherine of Aragon, who had unwittingly held Anne and Henry together, Anne knew that she was in a worse position than ever. Anne was always a great politician and she was determined to fight but, in February 1536, she knew that the cards were heavily stacked against her and that all the enemies she had made were lining up together in an attempt to bring her down.

CHAPTER 15

Sick and Tired of the Concubine

Anne's miscarriage at the end of January 1536 put her in a precarious position and she was well aware of the danger that she might be put away as Catherine of Aragon had been, due to her lack of a son. Henry's reaction to Anne's miscarriage must have terrified her and Anne would have been aware throughout the early months of 1536, that her influence over her husband was fast slipping away and she tried everything she could to stop it.

Anne spent some time in seclusion following her miscarriage and, on her return to court, she found herself surrounded by rumour and speculation. According to Chapuys in February 1536 'for more than three months this king has not spoken ten times to the Concubine, and that when she miscarried he scarcely said anything to her'. While this is likely to have been an exaggeration, the fact that such rumours were flying around court must have been difficult for her. Anne had spent nearly ten years as the object of Henry's devotion and, while this had waned somewhat following their marriage, he had never shown any signs of beginning a relationship as important to him as that with Anne. In early 1536, Anne, along with everyone else at court, would have been aware that Henry had a new love.

Anne had been aware that Henry had begun an affair with Jane Seymour before her miscarriage and, as before, she erupted into jealousy. Henry had given his new love a locket containing his picture which she wore proudly around her neck. This was too much for Anne and, on seeing it, she tore it from the lady's neck so fiercely that she hurt her hand. Anne was angry with Henry and furious with his mistress and she had already claimed that the sight of this lady on Henry's knee had caused her miscarriage. While Anne's love for Henry had probably evaporated as quickly as his love for her once they experienced the realities of married life, she knew that she needed him and she knew that she had set a dangerous precedent. By early 1536, with no son and a record of miscarriages beginning to resemble that of Catherine of Aragon, Anne was very aware of the danger of the appearance of another Anne Boleyn in the king's affections. Henry had had mistresses before of course, which Anne had barely been able to tolerate, but soon after her miscarriage she would have realised that Henry's new love, Jane Seymour, was of a very different mettle to his more casual mistresses and that, using Anne's own example, she was insisting on marriage or nothing.

In 1536 Jane Seymour was in her late twenties and a lady in Anne's household. By all accounts, she was no beauty or wit and the fact that no marriage had been arranged for her suggests that she was considered no great prospect on the marriage market. While she is often portrayed as a woman of low intelligence and little ambition, in reality Jane Seymour was a very great danger to Anne and she was intelligent enough to know how to behave in order to attract and hold the king. She also accepted coaching from others in her attempt to become the next Anne Boleyn. By March 1536, Jane and her supporters were well aware of the king's interest in her and she sought to portray herself as the exact opposite to Anne in order to hold the king's interest. While Anne had been outspoken and fascinating during Henry's courtship of her, Jane was meek and mild and conscious of her honour, all characteristics carefully chosen in order to present an appealing contrast to Anne for the king. Jane played this role to perfection and, according to Chapuys, she was given the perfect opportunity to prove her virtue when Henry:

'Sent her a purse full of sovereigns, and with it a letter, and that the young lady, after kissing the letter, returned it unopened to the messenger, and throwing herself on her knees before him, begged the said messenger that he would pray the king on her part to consider that she was a gentlewoman of good and honourable parents, without reproach, and that she had no greater riches in the world than her honour, which she would not injure for a thousand deaths, and that if he wished to make her some present in money she begged it might be when God enabled her to make some honourable marriage'.

This was the performance of Jane's life and it immediately attracted the king's interest, as Anne's own refusal to become his mistress had done before. Jane's new protestations of modesty were in direct contrast to her earlier behaviour with the king and it seems likely that, until Anne's miscarriage, the role she had attempted to gain was that of Henry's mistress. Following the miscarriage, Anne still had no son to secure her position and Jane and her supporters realised that the role of queen was once again potentially available.

Jane's message to the king certainly had the desired effect on Henry and his 'love and desire towards the said lady was wonderfully increased'. Henry, pleased at the contrast he saw between Jane and Anne, swore that he loved her honourably and sent a message to Jane telling her that he would now only speak to her in the presence of a member of her family to prove his honourable intentions towards her. This was exactly what Jane Seymour wanted to hear and a few days later Cromwell obligingly moved from his rooms at court which were conveniently connected to Henry's by means of a secret staircase. Jane's eldest brother, Edward Seymour, and his wife moved into the apartments, allowing Henry unfettered access to his new sweetheart. Before long, Henry was also writing Jane love letters, as he had previously done for Anne. One letter survives and, while it is not as passionate as Henry's letters to Anne in 1527, it does show clearly that the king now had a new love:

'My dear friend and mistress,
The bearer of these few lines from thy entirely devoted servant will deliver into thy fair hands a token of my affection for thee, hoping you will keep it for ever in your sincere love for me. Advertising you that there is a ballad made lately of great derision against me, which if you go abroad much and is seen by you I pray you pay no manner of regard to it. I am not at present informed who is the setter forth of this malignant writing, but if he is found he shall be straightly punished for it. For the things ye lacked I have minded my lord to supply them to you as soon as he can buy them. Thus hoping shortly to receive you in these arms. I end for the present.
Your own loving servant and sovereign. HR'.

Jane always continued to portray herself as a virtuous maiden and Chapuys pointed out in one of his dispatches that she:

'has been well taught for the most part by those intimate with the king, who hate the Concubine, that she must by no means comply with the King's wishes except by way of marriage; in which she is quite firm. She is also advised to tell the king boldly how his marriage is detested by the people, and none consider it lawful'.

Anne still had her supporters at court and she was fully aware of Jane Seymour. According to Chapuys, this sent her into an 'intense rage', and there is no doubt that Anne saw through Jane's professions of virtue. Just as Henry had been blind to any reports of Anne's imperfections early in their courtship, in 1536 he was blind to the evidence that Jane had set her heart on being queen as firmly as Anne herself had done. In early 1536 Anne no longer had sufficient influence over Henry to have Jane sent away and she was forced to sit and grit her teeth and hope that Jane would simply disappear, as Catherine of Aragon had no doubt done with her.

While Jane Seymour was herself as ambitious as Anne had been, she also quickly built a strong party around her. In March, Henry made Edward Seymour a member of his privy chamber and Jane's family were helping to coach her for her role as a future queen. Anne had also made many enemies during her time as queen and these disparate groups quickly fell in together behind Jane Seymour as a potential replacement for Anne. Chapuys was approached by his friend, the Marchioness of Exeter, to take action on behalf of Princess Mary and carefully weighed the situation before committing himself, writing to Charles V that:

'The said Marchioness would like that I or someone else, on the part of your Majesty, should assist in the matter, and certainly it appears to me that if it succeed, it will be a great thing both for the security of the Princess and to remedy the heresies here, of which the Concubine is the cause and principal nurse, and also to pluck the King from such an abominable and more than incestuous marriage. The Princess would be very happy, even if she were excluded from her inheritance by male issue'.

The addition of Mary's and imperial support to Jane's cause was dangerous to Anne and worse was to come when Thomas Cromwell also set himself behind Jane in an attempt to oust Anne.

Anne could never have foreseen that such different parties as the Seymours, Mary and the imperial interests and Cromwell could ever join together and she therefore can never have realised just how dangerous her position was in early 1536, for all the whispering that surrounded her. She and Cromwell both had a shared interest in reform and they had been, if not allies exactly, proponents of the same cause. Cromwell, as the shrewd politician that he was, also recognised the need to serve the king's every whim, and friendship with the king's wife had formed part of that policy. Following Anne's miscarriage and the rise of Jane Seymour, friendship with Anne would have looked a lot less necessary to Thomas Cromwell.

A contemporary of Anne, Alexander Ales, who was present at court during Anne's last few months as queen, later claimed that Cromwell and Anne became enemies when Anne discovered that he was using religious reform in order to benefit his own financial interests. Anne was passionate about the reform and there may be some truth in Ales's claim. It seems more likely that Cromwell and Anne had simply never been the firm allies that they were supposed to be. Anne had always found Cromwell a useful servant and she may not have realised that, while he was happy to do her bidding when she was in high favour, as the wind began to change he showed himself to be fully the king's man. Certainly, by 1 April 1536 word had reached Chapuys that Anne and Cromwell were on bad terms and that a new marriage for Henry was spoken about.

Chapuys was certainly happy to exploit the division between Anne and Cromwell and in late March he dined with Cromwell, telling him that:

'I had for some time forborne to visit him that he might not incur suspicion of his mistress [Anne] for the talk he had previously had with me, well remembering that he had previously told me that she would like to see his head cut off. This I could not forget for the love I bore him; and I would not but wish him a more gracious mistress and one more grateful for the inestimable services he had done the king, and that he must beware of enraging her, else he must never expect perfect reconciliation, in which case I hoped he would see it better than did the Cardinal'.

Cromwell had been a member of Wolsey's household at the time of his fall and he well remembered the enmity of Anne towards the Cardinal and her ability to bring him down. Anne was often given to rages and she would scream and shout at people who displeased her. It is easy to see how she could have told Cromwell that she would have his head in one of her outbursts, a comment that she may have made to those who angered her on other occasions. The difference was that in 1536 she was in a uniquely vulnerable position. She was as sonless as Catherine of Aragon and, like her predecessor, she had lost much of the king's affection. When Anne called for Cromwell's head, it may only have served to set the clever minister thinking about ways to ensure his own safety, even if that was at the cost of the queen's head instead.

In their conversation, Chapuys attempted to sound Cromwell out and discover exactly where the minister's sympathies lay. When he spoke of Henry's marriage to Anne, Cromwell stopped him and said that 'he had never been cause of this marriage, although, seeing the king determined upon it, he had smoothed the way'. While the pair spoke, Chapuys noticed that Cromwell had his hand over his mouth in an attempt to either stop himself smiling or to conceal a smile that was already there. Through his smile, Cromwell insisted that Henry was committed to his marriage and intended to live chastely with Anne. Cromwell's demeanour made it very clear to Chapuys that this was not, in fact, the case.

Although by March 1536, Henry certainly had no plans to live chastely with Anne, he was still very far from deciding to abandon his marriage and probably hoped that he would be able to persuade Jane Seymour to become his mistress. Henry had defied the Pope and the emperor in order to marry Anne and even after her miscarriage he was still committed to her as queen. The death of Catherine of Aragon in January had allowed both Anne and Henry to hope for a reconciliation with the emperor and Henry was determined that Catherine's nephew would recognise the validity of his marriage.

Charles was certainly still determined that his aunt's honour should not be damaged and he wrote to Chapuys in March on the subject, stating that his ambassador should not 'treat anything to the prejudice of the late Queen's honour, or her [Mary's] legitimacy or right to the succession'. Charles had also recognised the prospect for friendship with England that was opened up by Catherine's death and he instructed Chapuys to discuss an alliance and to find out what Anne would agree to. If Anne could have seen this letter, she would have been pleased to find this tacit acknowledgment of her presence by Catherine's powerful nephew and by 1536 she was certainly ready to attempt to enter into an imperial alliance if one were possible. She would also have been concerned to see that, while Charles ordered Chapuys to consider Anne, he also instructed his ambassador to press the king to remarry if this was found to be his preference. Charles was prepared to do business with Anne if it would secure an alliance with England, but he was very far from being in favour of such a course.

Anne saw the proffered Imperial alliance as a means of re-establishing her position at court in April 1536 and she was happy to attempt some reconciliation with the emperor. Henry was also determined that Charles should recognise his marriage and on Easter Sunday he instructed Cromwell to ask Chapuys to visit Anne and kiss her. This would have shown the world that the emperor recognised Anne as queen but Chapuys, who had always refused to meet personally with Anne, could not bring himself to agree to this, refusing to greet the woman who would always be to him, the Concubine. Both Anne and Henry expected this refusal and while in happier times Anne would have railed against it, she and Henry conceived a scheme to force Chapuys to finally recognise her. In spite of his refusal to meet Anne, Chapuys still found himself in high favour on Easter day and:

'Was conducted to mass by Lord Rochford, the Concubine's brother, and when the king came to the offering there was a great concourse of people partly to see how the Concubine and I behaved to each other. She was courteous enough, for when I was behind the door by which she entered, she returned, merely to do me reverence as I did her. After mass the king went to dine at the Concubine's lodging'.

Anne deliberately waited until her brother had manoeuvred Chapuys behind a door so that he had no chance to escape without finally acknowledging her as queen. This was a great victory for Anne and, at long last, she had achieved the recognition of Catherine's family of her rights as queen. It was to be the last victory of both Anne's reign and of her life and for all the hope it gave her, she was still filled with foreboding.

Anne had followed Henry in publicly rejoicing at the death of Catherine of Aragon in January and, to a certain extent, she must have been glad to finally be rid of her rival as queen. However, Anne was also no fool and she was well aware of just how exposed Catherine's death in reality left her. There must have been many times when Anne wished that Catherine and her daughter would simply disappear but she also recognised that Catherine's continued existence had forced the king to remain committed to his second marriage. If Henry were to put Anne away during Catherine's lifetime, pressure for him to take his first wife back would have been almost overwhelming. Most of Europe and many people in England did not recognise Henry's second marriage as valid and, with the death of Catherine, he was widely held to be free to marry again, regardless of Anne's position. While Anne put on a defiant face in public, she was no fool and she would have heard the rumours flying around court and trembled.

Following Anne's miscarriage, the English court was certainly full of rumours. These tended to centre on Anne's fertility and in February it was reported that Anne was unable to conceive a child and that Elizabeth was a changeling and the miscarried son a supposition. Anne probably attempted to laugh off rumours such as this, but they were widespread and they must have been both frustrating and deeply worrying to her. There were even claims that she had not been pregnant at all and had merely claimed that she had miscarried a son so that the king would think she was at least capable of conceiving a male heir. The much later report of Nicholas Sander also stated that Anne gave birth to a shapeless mass of flesh rather than a stillborn son in January. While there is no evidence to suggest this was the case, it does demonstrate just how embellished the rumours became as they piled down upon the beleaguered Anne.

By late April 1536 Anne was fully aware of just how low she stood in Henry's favour. Henry was, by then, intending to marry Jane Seymour as soon as he could be rid of Anne and, on 29 April he showed this clearly by appointing Sir Nicholas Carey, a supporter of Jane, as a Knight of the Garter in preference to George Boleyn. As Chapuys gleefully reported, 'the Concubine has not had sufficient influence to get it for her brother'. This was a major blow to Anne and the entire Boleyn faction and Anne decided to take decisive action to disprove the rumours and offer Henry the only proof of her fertility she had. At some point near the end of April, Anne took Elizabeth in her arms and held her out to Henry as he looked down from an open window at Greenwich Palace. This was Anne's last attempt to reawaken Henry's love for her and it failed utterly. While, for Anne, Elizabeth was the proof that she could bear a healthy child, for Henry she was only proof of his wife's betrayal in her failure to provide him with the son she had promised him. Angry words were spoken between the couple and Anne then moved away defeated. It was probably the last time she saw her daughter.

While at the end of April 1536 Anne was aware that she had lost the king's love, she cannot have foreseen the rapidity of her fall, for all the whispers that surrounded her. Anne had always been a politician as well as a queen, forming factions and policies as actively as Henry's ministers. By late April 1536 Henry had decided to bring her political influence to an end and had accepted that Anne was as much of a problem to him as Catherine of Aragon had once been. On 24 April 1536, a commission was set up to investigate certain treasons and, with official approval for an investigation into Anne's conduct, it was only a matter of time before she fell from power. As Chapuys sent to tell Mary on 29 April, she should be of good cheer, 'for the king was already as sick and tired of the Concubine as could be'. On 1 May 1536, Henry and the rest of Anne's enemies were ready to strike her down.

CHAPTER 16

Turned Trust to Treason

Anne suspected that she had lost Henry's love and was being conspired against in April 1536 but she can never have imagined the speed with which she would fall. She probably hoped that, if only she could reawaken Henry's obsession with her, she would be safe and might finally bear him a son. Anne can never have imagined just how dangerous her situation was in April 1536 but, on 30 April, Cromwell was ready to strike.

On 30 April 1536 Mark Smeaton, a young musician in Anne's household, was invited to dine with Cromwell at his house at Stepney. This was a flattering invitation for Smeaton, who was not gently born and he went gladly, probably hoping for some preferment from the king's chief minister. He was completely unsuspecting when he arrived at Stepney and, rather than being offered a meal, found himself arrested by Cromwell's men and taken to the Tower for interrogation. Smeaton must have been terrified and there were rumours that he was racked or subjected to some other torture. By the following morning, he had confessed to committing adultery with Anne and provided both Cromwell and the king with the means to take the final action against the queen.

Smeaton was a member of Anne's household but he was so lowly that she is unlikely to have noted his disappearance. Even if she did, she would not have thought anything of it and may simply have been annoyed that he was neglecting his duties towards her. She did not imagine just how dangerous his disappearance was to her and it was an entirely unsuspecting Anne who attended the May Day jousts at Greenwich the following day. The jousts were a great affair, attended by the entire court with Henry sitting close to Anne. Anne may have hoped to be able to speak to her husband at the jousts and her mood was lighter than it had been for several weeks as she watched her brother and other gentlemen, including Henry Norris, a favourite of the king, and Thomas Wyatt, in the jousts. Anne noticed nothing amiss as she sat in the gallery and, as she watched, she dropped her handkerchief to one of the jousters to allow him to wipe his face. Anne had always been flirtatious with men and sought the admiration of the gentlemen of court. She would have seen nothing unusual in her action and she, along with the rest of the court, was perturbed when Henry suddenly got to his feet and left the jousts without saying a word.

Henry took only six attendants with him when he left Greenwich, including Henry Norris, and he rode swiftly towards the palace of Westminster. According to the account of George Constantine, Norris's servant, Henry insisted on riding at the head of the group beside Norris and 'all the waye as I heard saye, had Mr Noryce in examinacyon and promised hym his pardon in case he wolde utter the trewth. But what so ever could be sayed or done, Mr Norice wold confess no thinge to the Kynge, where vpon he was committed to the towre in the mornynge'. Although no details of Henry's questions survive, they can only have been about Norris's relationship with Anne. With Smeaton and Norris in custody, it was decided that the next suspect to be apprehended would be Anne Boleyn herself.

Little evidence concerning the charges against Anne and the men with whom she was accused survives and it is therefore impossible to fully judge the basis for the charges and the evidence. It appears from the surviving evidence that the source of the accusations come from evidence given by four women; Lady Wingfield, Lady Worcester, Lady Rochford and Anne Boleyn herself. The judge, Sir John Spelman, who sat on the bench during Anne's trial, noted that Anne had originally been accused by Lady Wingfield. Lady Wingfield had died in either 1533 or 1534 but she left a deathbed statement which apparently accused Anne of being morally lax. Although this statement does not survive, it seems likely that it related to some premarital affair on Anne's part. As already noted, the usually proud Anne wrote to Lady Wingfield in very subservient tones whilst she was still Lady Marquis of Pembroke and it is almost certain that Lady Wingfield knew a secret about the queen that Anne was desperate should never be revealed. Given the attention paid to Henry Percy at the time of Anne's fall and, also, the fact that Anne may have considered herself contracted to him, it is reasonable to speculate that Lady Wingfield's confession stated that Anne and Percy had consummated their relationship, something that Anne would have been very loath to have revealed to the king. When Lady Wingfield's statement was finally brought to Cromwell and the king in early 1536, it was enough to cast doubt on Anne's morality and for further investigations to be carried out. While a lack of premarital chastity was a ground for divorce, it was certainly not treason and Anne was also the subject of a far more damning allegation by the Countess of Worcester.

According to a letter written by John Husee to Lady Lisle a few days after Anne's death 'the first accusers, the Lady Worcester, and Nan Cobham, with one maid more. But Lady Worcester was the first ground'. Lady Worcester was a member of Anne's household and she was noted for her loose morals. According to a letter written by Lady Worcester to Cromwell in March 1537, Anne had lent her £100, a vast sum, for some purpose which she did not specify but which Lady Worcester was 'very loath it should come to my lord my husband's knowledge, which is and hath been utterly ignorant both of the borrowing and using of the said hundred pounds. And if he should now have knowledge thereof, I am in doubt how he will take it'. It appears that Lady Worcester had a lover and in early 1536, her brother, Sir Anthony Browne, berated her for her immoral conduct. In her anger, Lady Worcester blurted out that she was not the worst and that her brother should look to the conduct of the queen herself. This was enough for Henry, seeking a way to be rid of Anne, to permit Cromwell to carry out an investigation into her conduct.

By early 1536, Cromwell and Anne were at odds, and the minister used any means at his disposal to produce evidence against her. According to Alexander Ales, who was at court during the last weeks of Anne's life, Cromwell's agents 'tempt her porter and serving men with bribes, there is nothing which they do not promise the ladies of her bedchamber. They affirm that the King hated the Queen, because she hath not presented him with an heir to the realm, nor was there any prospect of her doing so'. These spies apparently searched out people willing to inform against the queen and one of those who testified was Anne's sister-in-law, Lady Rochford, who was apparently angry with her husband and 'seeking of his blood'. She claimed that Anne and George laughed at the king's clothes and discussed his impotence. She also told Cromwell that George had questioned the paternity of Elizabeth. It is unclear whether Lady Rochford acted under duress or not, but her words were damning and, with the help of the three ladies, Henry and Cromwell were ready to arrest Anne herself on 2 May. Anne's own role in the accusations occurred soon afterwards.

Anne spent an anxious night at Greenwich following Henry's abrupt departure from the jousts and she may have suspected that he had spent the night with Jane Seymour or one of the other ladies of the court. A veil of silence had been placed around her and she would not have known of either Smeaton's arrest nor Norris's interrogation until her uncle, the Duke of Norfolk, with several other members of the king's council came to arrest her on the morning of 2 May. When Anne was told of the charges, she immediately exclaimed that she was wronged and begged to see the king, but she was not permitted to do so. Anne spent much of that day being interrogated before being taken to the Tower of London at 5pm that evening. No details of Anne's interrogation survive, but she was certainly terrified. Anne had known that she was rapidly losing Henry's love, but she can never have imagined herself as a prisoner in the Tower. As she arrived at the Tower, her self-composure gave way and 'she fell downe on her knees before the said lords, beseeching God to help her as she was not giltie of her accusement, and also desired the saide lords to bessech the kinge's grace to be good unto her, and so they left her prisoner'. By the time that she had arrived at the Tower, Anne knew that she was accused of adultery and she had heard that her brother had also been taken to the Tower that same day. Anne would never again leave the Tower and all her composure had gone. As she entered the Tower she asked the lieutenant of the Tower, William Kingston, 'shall I go in to a dungyn?' Kingston assured her that she would be lodged in the royal apartments where she had slept before her coronation, and she was led away, attended by only four ladies selected for her by either the king or by Cromwell.

In the first few days of her imprisonment, Anne was a nervous wreck, desperately trying to work out why she had been imprisoned by the husband who had once pursued her so obsessively. To Kingston's confusion, she alternated between weeping and laughing and she also spoke unguardedly, apparently trying to make sense of what could have caused her fall. On her arrival in the Tower, Anne asked Kingston why she was in the Tower and he said he did not know. She then asked him about her brother, pleading 'O [where ys] my swet brod'er?'. Anne then said that she thought she would be accused with three men, presumably referring to her brother,

Henry Norris and Mark Smeaton and she cried out '[O Nor]es, hast thow accused me, thow ar in the Towre with me, & [thou and I shal]l dy to gether and, Marke, thou art here to. O my mother, [thou wilt dy] for sorow'. Anne then piteously asked Kingston '[shall I dy] with yowt just[ice]'. Kingston replied that 'the porest sugett the kyng [hath had justis]' and Anne burst out laughing.

Anne had always been proud of her intelligence and self-possession, but in her first few days at the Tower she was a piteous sight, desperately turning over any incident in her head that could have caused her to fall so far. According to Kingston, soon after her arrival in the Tower:

> 'The queen spake of West[on that she] had spoke to hym by cause he dyd love hyr kynswoma[n Mrs Shelton and that s]he sayd he loves not hys wyf and he made anser to hyr [again that he] loved won in hyr howse better then them bothe[; she asked him who is that? To which he answered] that it ys your selfe; and then she defied hym'.

Francis Weston who was, like Norris, a member of Henry's privy council, had not previously come to the attention of Anne's investigators, but Anne's words were enough to damn him and that night he also found himself a prisoner in the Tower.

Anne was clearly thinking hard to find any incident that could have caused her arrest, and she also spoke of Mark Smeaton in the Tower. Anne told Kingston that Smeaton was the worst cherished of any man in her household because he was not a gentleman. According to Kingston, she then stated 'bot he wase never in m[y chamber but at Winchestr, and] ther she sent for hym to ple[y on the virginals, for there my] logyng was [above the kings]'. She then continued:

> 'For I never spake with hym syns, bot apon Saturday before May day, and then I found hym standing in the ronde wyndo in my chamber of presens, and I asked why he wase so sad, and he answered and sayd it was now mater, and then she sayd, yu may not loke to have me speke to you as I shuld do to anobull man, by cause you be aninferer person. No, no, madam, aloke sufficed me, and thus far you well'.

Anne considered Smeaton as beneath her notice and the idea that he might be her lover would have made her laugh. She also spoke to Kingston of her brother and, when it was confirmed that he was also in the Tower, she replied 'I am very glad, said sh[e that we] bothe be so ny together'. For

Anne, these were probably innocent words, but her mention of Norris, Weston, Smeaton and George Boleyn were all noted and reported to Cromwell and used as evidence against her.

Norris, Weston, Smeaton and George were not the only men arrested during the early days of Anne's imprisonment and William Brereton, another member of Henry's privy council was also taken to the Tower as one of Anne's alleged lovers. Brereton is a particularly unlikely choice for a lover. In 1536, he was in his late forties and the fact that Anne never mentioned him in the Tower suggests that he was not well known to her. Some of Anne's own contemporaries also speculated that he was innocent and George Constantine, who knew Brereton personally, asserted that 'yf any of them was innocent, it was he. For other he was innocente or else he dyed worst of them all'. Constantine spoke to Brereton on the day of his arrest and he made no sign that he was expecting to be caught up in the matter himself. Brereton was married to the sister of the Earl of Worcester and it is therefore possible that it was Lady Worcester who first mentioned his name. In the suspicious days following Anne's arrest, a mention was all that it took and Thomas Wyatt was also committed to the Tower due to his past links with Anne. A further man, Sir Richard Page, was also arrested, although his connection with Anne is entirely unclear.

As the days wore on, Anne collected herself a little and was able to complain to Kingston one day after supper that she 'was creuely handeled'. She then continued that:

'To be a queen and creueley handeled as was never sene; bot I [think the king] dose it to prove me, and dyd lawth with all and was very mery, and th[ein she said I shall have just]ists; and then I sayde have now dowt ther[in]; then she sayd yf hony man [accuse me I can say bot n]ay, & thay can bring now wytnes'.

Anne simply could not believe that the king who had loved her so passionately could desire her death. She also told Kingston that she wished that she could see her bishops as they would go to the king and speak for her. If Anne believed that the men that she had helped promote to bishoprics were truly 'her' bishops, she was mistaken and even Cranmer maintained public support for the king.

Anne had been instrumental in securing Cranmer's appointment as archbishop and she would certainly have included him amongst 'her' bishops. She cannot have known that Cranmer, on hearing the news of Anne's fall, had written to the king disassociating himself firmly from Anne in a bid to save both himself and the future of the religious reform. Cranmer wrote:

> 'If it be true what is openly reported of the queen's grace, if men had a right estimation of things, they should not esteem any part of your grace's honour to be touched thereby, but her honour only to be clearly disparaged. And I am in such a perplexity, that my mind is clean amazed, for I never had a better opinion in woman than I had of her, which maketh me think she should not be culpable. Now I think that your grace best knoweth, that next unto your grace I was most bound unto her of all creatures living. Wherefore I must humbly beseech your grace to suffer me in that which both God's law, nature, and her kindness, bindeth me, unto that I may (with your grace's favour) wish and pray for her. And from what condition your grace, of your only mere goodness, took her, and set the crown upon her head, I repute him not your grace's faithful servant and subject, nor true to the realm, that would not desire the offence to be without mercy punished, to the example of all others. And as I loved her not a little, for the love I judged her to bear towards God and his holy Gospel, so, if she be proved culpable, there is not one that loveth God and his Gospel that will ever favour her, but must hate her, for then there never was creature in our time that so slandered the Gospel. And God hath sent her this punishment, for that she frequently hath progressed the Gospel in her mouth, and not in her heart and deed, and though she hath offended, so that she hath deserved never to be reconciled to your grace's favour, yet God Almighty hath manifoldly declared his goodness towards your grace, and never offended you'.

Anne would have agreed with Cranmer's attempts to preserve the religious reform at all costs, but she cannot have been happy to find that she was to be abandoned by those whom she thought she could count on for support. In reality, Cranmer may not have abandoned Anne quite as fully as he assured the king and, according to Alexander Ales, he said sadly following Anne's death that 'she who has been the queen of England upon earth will to-day become a queen in heaven'. Cranmer then burst into tears. Anne may have had his private sympathy but he could not support her publicly and most people in England were prepared to think the worst of her following her arrest.

Whether Anne was guilty or innocent of the charges against her has been debated for centuries. Certainly, at the time of her imprisonment great attempts were made to secure further confessions and both Cromwell and Henry were disappointed that only Smeaton ever confessed. Anne's poor reputation meant that people were prepared to believe almost anything of her and Jane Dormer, a friend of Anne's stepdaughter, Mary, believed that Anne had committed adultery with George, Weston, Norris, Brereton and Smeaton in an attempt to conceive a son. The contemporary *Chronicle of Henry VIII,* also claimed that Anne was guilty, stating that she 'ostentatiously tried to attract the best-looking men and best dancers to be found'. According to the *Chronicle*, Anne heard that Mark Smeaton was a good player and dancer and she sent for him to play for her. Once Mark had played, Anne danced with him and found he danced so well that she 'at once fell in love with him'. The Chronicler was in no doubt about Anne's guilt, referring also to Norris and Brereton as Anne's 'minions'. However, the Chronicler was not a member of the court and would only have based his assessment on Anne's reputation and the rumours that surrounded her fall, as would Jane Dormer.

Chapuys also believed that adultery had truly been discovered and that Anne's arrest was the judgment of God. This was also the official response put about by Cromwell and, on 14 May, the minister wrote that 'the queen's incontinent living was so rank and common that the ladies of her privy chamber could not conceal it. It came to the ears of some of the Council, who told his Majesty, although, with great fear'. Cromwell claimed that a plot had been discovered between Anne and her lovers against the king's life and Henry himself also went along with the pretence. In what can only be described as a staged scene, on the night of Anne's arrest, Henry's illegitimate son, the Duke of Richmond, came to him to bid him goodnight. According to Chapuys, 'the king began to weep, saying that he and his sister, meaning the Princess, were greatly bound to God for having escaped the hands of that accursed whore, who had determined to poison them'. Even Chapuys could not help noting that Henry had lodged Jane Seymour nearby and that he was attempting to cover up his affections for his new love.

Most people in England were prepared to believe the worst about Anne but among those people at court it is possible that there was a little more unease. According to Alexander Ales, even Anne's enemies recognised that the evidence was only circumstantial and they said that:

'It is no new thing, said they, that the King's Chamberlains should dance with the ladies in the bedchamber. Nor can any proof of adultery be collected from the fact that the queen's brother took her by the hand and led her into the dance among the other ladies, or handed her to another, especially if that person was one of the royal chamberlains. For it is a usual custom throughout the whole of Britain that ladies married and unmarried, even the most coy, kiss not only a brother but any honourable person, even in public'.

Those who heard the actual evidence against Anne and her 'lovers' may have been a little uneasy.

Although Cromwell was the driving force behind the investigation into Anne, he could not have acted without the approval of the king. By April 1536 Henry was no longer committed to his marriage to Anne and he was looking towards a new future with Jane Seymour. While Anne was certainly accused by Lady Wingfield and Lady Worcester, these accusations only provided the basis of the investigations; the decision to charge Anne and her 'lovers' was entirely Henry's. What is apparent from the accusations surrounding Anne is that she enjoyed dancing and even flirtations with men but it is simply inconceivable that she would have found the opportunity, and the privacy, to commit adultery with five men. The simple fact is that by April 1536, Henry wanted rid of Anne. He wanted to ensure that the marriage ended quickly given the difficulties that he had had with Catherine of Aragon, and he wanted to ensure that his children by a new wife would be entirely legitimate. By accusing Anne of adultery, a charge many people were prepared to believe given her poor reputation, he was able to ensure that there would be no discarded wife threatening his new marriage. Henry's love for Anne was dead and he could be ruthless to those who fell out of favour, as Anne's enemy, Wolsey, had found. Even before her trial, Henry did not envisage Anne ever being released and, on 13 May, her household was disbanded on the command of the king. A contemporary of Anne, George Cavendish, who fully believed in Anne's guilt, claimed that she had 'turned trust to treason' but, in reality, it was Henry who had done this, not Anne. As Anne gradually recovered her self-possession, she realised that her husband had entirely forsaken her and she knew that the result of her trial was a foregone conclusion.

CHAPTER 17

The Lady in the Tower

Anne spent nearly two weeks in the Tower before her trial, agonising over everything that had happened to her and dreading the days ahead. She was not permitted to see Henry, nor the men with whom she was accused and, instead, she was kept closely watched in the royal apartments in the Tower. From what little she was told, Anne began to piece together the accusations against her and she prepared to defend herself, although she would have known that the result of her trial was a foregone conclusion.

By 12 May 1536, the charges against Anne and her alleged lovers had been prepared and Norris, Brereton, Weston and Smeaton were taken under guard to Westminster Hall for their trial. On their arrival, the four men faced the king's commissioners and were charged 'that they had violated and had carnal knowledge of the said queen, each by himself at separate times'. This was the first time that the charges against Anne and the men had been publicly stated and the words must have sent a chill through the hearts of the men as the court was opened. It is unclear whether any evidence was presented to the men and they would have been allowed no counsel nor witnesses to speak in their defence. Details of the trial are sketchy but according to Sir John Spelman, one of the judges who oversaw the proceedings, 'Mark [Smeaton] confessed that he had [had] carnal knowledge of the queen three times. Norris, Brereton and Weston pleaded not guilty, but were found guilty, and had judgment to be drawn, hanged, and beheaded and quartered'. Following the guilty verdict, the four terrified men were returned to the Tower from which they would never again emerge.

Anne would have known of the men's trial even without any official announcement. Although a prisoner, she was kept in the palace in the Tower rather than the dungeons and she may have watched from her window as the men were led out of the Tower and when they returned. Anne knew that, even though there was no proof against any of them, they would be found guilty, and she also realised what the ramifications were for her own trial. The four men had been convicted of adultery with her and with a guilty verdict against them, there was no way that she could ever be acquitted. None the less, Anne fully intended to defend herself and she was glad to hear that the men, with the exception of Smeaton, had refused to admit to any crime. It seems probable that Smeaton, whose confession may well have been extracted under torture, had been promised his life if he would confess, a fact of which Anne may have been aware.

As members of the nobility, Anne and her brother were afforded the special privilege of being tried within the Tower itself and, on the morning of 15 May, Anne prepared herself for her appearance before her peers. Anne had always known how to make the best of herself and she dressed carefully for her trial. England had never before seen a queen tried and a special scaffold had been built in the hall at the Tower to ensure there were places for all those required to attend. According to an anonymous account of Anne's trial, the nobility assembled first:

> 'The Duke of Norfolke sittinge vnder the cloath of state, the Lord Chauncellour on his right hand, and the Duke of Suffolke on his lefte, the Earle of Surrey, sonne of the Duke of Norfolke, sittinge directly before his Father, a degree lower, as Earle Marshall of England; to whome were adioyned 26 other Peeres, and among them the Queenes Father, by whome shee was to be tryed'.

Tudor England was no place for family sentiment and neither Norfolk nor Thomas Boleyn, for all the differences that they had had with Anne, can have relished their roles at her trial. Anne's old suitor, Henry Percy, Earl of Northumberland, was also compelled by his rank to attend Anne's trial, although the strain affected his already failing health and he was forced to leave George's trial due to illness.

Once all the peers had assembled, the king's commission was read and Anne was led into the hall. She was a prisoner but she was still accorded the respect due to her as the king's wife and Anne would have been pleased to find a special chair waiting for her which had been made expressly for the purpose of her trial. It was a small comfort, and Anne quickly focussed her mind on the charges laid against her. She had no counsel and could call no witnesses and was solely responsible for her own defence.

Surviving details of Anne's trial are sparse. Following her arrival in the hall, the charges against her were read. Although Anne had heard rumours of what she was charged with, this was the first time that they were set out clearly to her and she may have laughed at the absurdity of the list of her offences. Sir John Spelman, who again sat on the bench at Anne's trial made a short note, setting out the charges against Anne and her 'lovers'. According to Spelman:

'The said queen and lord [George Boleyn], and the other four, were indicted twice (once in the county of Kent, and again in the county of Middlesex) for one same treason, but it was supposed at different times and places. And the points against the queen were that she procured the said lord her brother and the other four to defile her and have carnal knowledge of her, and that they did so; and that they conspired the king's death, for she said that the king should never have her heart and she said to each of the four by himself that he loved him more than the others, and this slandered the issue which was begotten between her and the king, which is made treason by the statute of the twenty-sixth year of the present king. And all the evidence was of bawdery and lechery, so that there was no such whore in the realm'.

Anne must have been horrified that the Act of Succession, which had been designed to protect both her and her children from slander should be used against her and, as each charge against her was read, she would have realised just how impatient Henry was to be rid of her, less than a decade after he had first fallen so passionately in love with her.

The list of specific charges levelled against Anne also survives from her trial. According to the indictment, Anne, 'despising her marriage, entertaining malice against the king, and following daily her frail and carnal lust, did falsely and traitorously procure by base conversations and kisses, touching, gifts, and other infamous incitations, divers of the king's daily and familiar servants to be her adulterers and concubines'. Anne was portrayed at her trial as, essentially, a nymphomaniac, desperate for the company of men. The commission even went so far as to offer specific dates for her crimes, for example stating that on 6 October 1534 she procured Henry Norris 'by sweet words, kisses, touches, and otherwise' and they committed adultery together six days later, as well as on several other occasions. The following year in November, according to the indictment, Anne 'procured and incited her own natural brother, George Boleyn, Lord Rocheford, gentleman of the privy chamber, to violate her, alluring him with her tongue in the said George's mouth, and the said George's tongue in hers, and also with kisses, presents, and jewels'. Anne and George 'despising the laws of God' committed incest on numerous occasions according to the charges and Anne was also charged with procuring the other three men on various days during her time as queen. Even more damagingly, Anne was also accused of conspiring for the death of the king with her lovers so that she would be free to marry one of them.

The charges against Anne were outrageous and she must have felt like laughing bitterly as she sat in the hall. Once they had been read, Anne stood to make her defence. No details of Anne's speech survive but she must have pointed out the absurdity of the charges in a society where the queen was never permitted to be alone. She may also have asserted her continuing love for the king although, by this point, Anne may well have begun to hate him. Whatever Anne did say, she certainly made an impression on everyone assembled. Henry's Chancellor, Wriothesley, commented that 'she made so wise and discreet aunsweres in all things layde against her, excusing herself with her words so clearlie, as though she had never bene faultic to the same'. The anonymous author of the account of Anne's trial was also impressed with her eloquence and stated that she, 'haueinge an excellent quick witt, and being a ready speaker, did so answeare to all obiections, that, had the Peeres given theire verdict according to the expectacion of the assembly, shee had beene acquitted'. Anne sat down knowing that she had done all she could but also knowing that it was not enough.

Following Anne's speech, the assembled peers, one by one, gave the verdict of guilty, as Anne would have known they would. She may have made eye contact with her father or Henry Percy as each peer gave the same answer in turn, aware that they were as trapped as she was. Even Anne's uncle, Norfolk, was touched by the knowledge that he would have to give judgment against his niece and there were tears in his eyes as he delivered the sentence. He had no choice but to continue and, turning to Anne, Norfolk declared that she had been found guilty of high treason. The only possible sentence for high treason was death and, for a woman, that meant burning. Anne must have steeled herself for her uncle's words, although she knew what was to come. She was probably as shocked as the rest of the assembly when Norfolk declared a dual sentence, that 'she should be burned or beheaded at the king's pleasure'. This sentence may have been devised by Henry to show that he did not intend Anne to suffer but, for Anne, it can have meant little and she knew as she was escorted back to her apartments in the Tower that she was condemned to die.

Once Anne had left the great hall, George was led in to face his judges. Like Anne, he knew that the result was inevitable although he may not yet have heard of his sister's conviction. George Boleyn would also have had an idea of what the charges against him would be and he probably listened calmly to the accusation that he had committed incest with his sister. According to Chapuys, the evidence presented for this charge was that 'he had been once found a long time with her'. This was the flimsiest of possible evidence and George contemptuously dismissed it when it was put to him. He was also charged, as Anne was, with having laughed at the king and his clothes. Given the fact that both Anne and George prided themselves on their cosmopolitan education and experience, this may well have been true and the stylish Anne may have attempted to teach Henry about dress in the early days of their relationship.

George batted away the more outrageous charges but there may have been truth in some of the other accusations levelled against him. According to Chapuys, George was handed a piece of paper during the course of his trial which he was instructed not to read out to the court. George however, contemptuously read from the paper, declaring to the court that it said that Anne had told his wife that the king was impotent. George must have been furious to find that his wife was one of the informants against him and it does seem likely that both he and Anne would have discussed the king's problem together. The report was widely believed and Chapuys wrote a few days after George's trial when discussing Jane Seymour's prospects that 'according to the account given by the Concubine, he [Henry] has neither vigour nor virtue'. Following the Act of Succession, such speculation was treason in that it impugned the king's issue and George also refused to answer the charge that he had called into question whether Elizabeth was, in fact, Henry's child. It seems likely that, in his conversations with Anne, George may indeed have joked that, if the king was impotent, then Elizabeth could not be his, and these words came back to haunt him.

There may have been some truth in the minor charges against George but the main charge of incest is completely improbable and George defended himself as eloquently as Anne had done before him. According to Chapuys, no great admirer of George, 'he replied so well that several of those present wagered 10 to 1 that he would be acquitted'. Like Anne, George's efforts were in vain and he was also convicted by the assembled peers and sentenced to die.

With the convictions of Anne, George, Norris, Brereton, Weston and Smeaton, only Thomas Wyatt and Sir Richard Page remained in the Tower unsure of their fate. It is unclear why no attempt was made to try Wyatt and Page as Anne's lovers and it may be that even the spurious evidence used against the other men could not be found in their cases. Certainly, rumours surrounded them as much as the other men. On 10 May, Cromwell wrote to Wyatt's father to assure him that his son's life was not in danger. While this was a comfort to Wyatt's family, much uncertainty still shrouded the two men left languishing in the Tower. Rumours flew around court and while, on 12 May, John Husee felt able to write that Wyatt and Page were expected to escape with their lives, on the next day he heard that both were going to be executed and that it was Weston who would survive. Even after the trials, the fate of everyone in the Tower was still shrouded in uncertainty.

Anne knew full well that she had not received justice in her trial and she may have written to Henry from the Tower expressing her anger. Following the fall of Thomas Cromwell in 1540, a letter was found amongst his papers inscribed from 'the Lady in the Tower' and purporting to be from Anne to Henry. While the letter is not in Anne's handwriting, it is possible that it was a copy of a genuine letter and that the original was destroyed by the king. The tone of the letter sounds like Anne and she began by telling the king that she would never acknowledge guilt where she had none, claiming that 'to speak a truth, never a prince had wife more loyal in all duty, and in all true affection, than you have ever found in Anne Bulen'. She also confirmed that she knew full well that 'the ground of my preferment being on no surer foundation than your grace's fancy, the least alteration was fit and sufficient (I knew) to draw that fancy to some other subject'. Anne continued, begging the king to give her a fair trial, which would presumably be more impartial than the mockery of a trial that she had already been through. In her request for an impartial trial she pointed out that:

'Then you shall see either my innocency cleared, your suspicions and conscience satisfied, the ignomity and slander of the world stopped, or my guilt openly declared, So that, whatever God and you may determine of, your grace may be freed from an open censure; and my offence being so lawfully proved, your grace may be at liberty, both before God and man, not only to execute worthy punishment on me as an unfaithful wife but to follow your affection already settled on that party for whose sake I am now as I am'

Anne blamed her enemies for the position in which she found herself. She also begged that the men with whom she was accused would not die on her behalf. If this letter was truly from Anne, and it may well have been, Henry made no response. He had no further use for the woman he had once loved so dearly and, on 17 May, Thomas Cranmer annulled Anne's marriage in a church court at Lambeth, based on her precontract with Henry Percy, declaring that she 'was never lawfull Queen of England'. Anne's pleas for clemency for her supposed lovers also fell on deaf ears.

Anne fully came to understand that she was to die on 17 May. On the same day that she ceased to be queen of England and Henry's wife, Anne's five convicted lovers were also executed. The five men were all taken out to die together as Anne watched from her window at the Tower. It may have been some comfort to her to know that the king, in his mercy, had commuted the sentences of the four gentlemen to simple beheading rather than the more painful death of hanging, drawing and quartering. Only Smeaton, who was no gentleman, would suffer that death and Anne may have felt that there was some justice in this since he was the only man to accuse her.

As was customary, the condemned men were permitted to make a speech on the scaffold and all would have known that, by convention, they were expected to recognise the justness of their approaching death. George gave a good speech as befitted his education, saying:

'Christian men, I am borne under the lawe, and judged under the lawe, and dye under the lawe, and the lawe hathe condemned me. Masters all, I am not come hether for to preche, but for to dye, for I have deserved to dye yf I had xx. lyves, more shamefully than can be devised for I am a wreched synnar, and I have synned shamefully, I have knowne no man so evell, and to reherse my synnes openly it were no pleasure to you to here them, nor get for me to reherse them, for God knowethe all; therefore, masters all, I pray you take hede by me, and especially my lords and gentlemen of the cowrte, the whiche I have bene amonge, take hede by me, and beware of suche a fall, and I pray to God the Fathar, the Sonne, and the Holy Ghoste, thre persons and one God, that my deathe may be an example unto you all, and beware, trust not in the vanitie of the worlde, and especially in the flateringe of the cowrte'.

George continued in a similar vein, recognising, as was expected, his worthiness to die, but never admitting guilt in the offences for which he died. Anne would have been glad to hear this. Norris, said very little on the scaffold but he also did not admit to the offences of which he died. Weston also refused to admit any guilt, saying 'I had thought to have lyved in abhominacion yet this twenty or thrittie yeres & then to have made amendes. I thought little it wold have come to this'. Brereton even went so far as to indicate that he was not guilty, declaring 'I have deserved to dye if it were a thousand deethes, but the cause wherefore I dye judge not: But yf ye judge, judge the best'. By denying his guilt, Brereton did not die a good death, as expected by his contemporaries, but he did get his point across. Smeaton said simply 'Masters I pray you all praye for me, for I have deserved the deeth', terrified to find that he had not, after all, been spared, in spite of his confession. Anne probably felt that he deserved death of all the men who died for her and when she was told of his words, she cried out 'did he not exoncrate me. Before he died, of the public infamy he laid on me? Alas! I fear his soul will suffer for it'. Anne heard all the details of the men's deaths and she also determined that she would die a good death.

Anne spent the last few days of her life preparing herself for death. She also took steps to show the world her innocence of the crimes of which she was convicted. According to Sir William Kingston, writing on 18 May 'I suppose she wyll declare hyr self to b[e a good] woman for all men bot for the kyng at the or of hyr de[th. For thys] morning she sent for me that I might be with hyr at [soche tyme] as she reysayved the gud lord to the in tent I shuld here hy[r speke as] towchyng her innosensy'. Anne did indeed declare her innocence both before and after receiving the sacrament, telling proof of her innocence in a woman as religious as Anne. Once she had made her point, Anne then spent her last hours on earth preparing for death, determined that she would not show anyone that she was beaten.

After declaring her innocence in front of Sir William Kingston, Anne summoned him again and said 'M. Kyngston,

I he[ar saye I shall] not dy affore none, & I am very sory ther fore; for I thowth [than to] be dede [an]d past my payne. I told hyr it shuld be now payne it w[as so sottel. And then she said I] hard say the executr was very gud, and I have a ly[ttle necke, and put he]r hand abowt it lawyng hartely'. Kingston was astounded by Anne's levity, writing that 'I have sen[e mony men &] also wemen executed and at they have bene in gre[te sorrowe, and to my knowle]ge thys lady hathe meche joye and plesur in dethe'. By 18 May, with her brother dead, her daughter bastardised and herself divorced and discredited, Anne may well have desired death. Equally, her levity may simply have been an attempt to show the world that she was still Anne Boleyn and still the most fascinating woman in England. Anne's conduct astounded her contemporaries and even Chapuys' reports show a certain grudging admiration. According to Chapuys, Anne spent the last evening of her life talking and jesting and even suggesting that her nickname would be 'Queen Anne Lack-Head'. Anne was defying the king in the only way she had left to her; by seeming to be happy in his treatment of her. It cannot have been entirely genuine and she must have spent her last night in an agony of apprehension as she prepared for her final big appearance.

On the morning of 19 May, most of Henry's council, the Dukes of Richmond and Suffolk, and many of the earls, lords and nobles in the kingdom, along with the mayor of London and the Aldermen and sheriffs assembled to watch Anne Boleyn die. It was almost the same crowd who had attended Anne at her coronation and she may have noticed the irony as she stepped out of the royal apartments, attended by her ladies. Anne walked over to the scaffold, maintaining her dignity and composure and seeming every inch the queen. Once on the scaffold, she turned to face the crowd and began her meticulously prepared speech, knowing that this would be the last act of her life:

'Good Christen people, I am come hether to dye, for according to the lawe and by the lawe I am iudged to dye, and therefore I wyll speake nothing against it. I am come hether to accuse no man, nor to speake any thing of that wherof I am accused and condemned to dye, but I pray God save the king and send him long to reigne over you, for a gentler nor a more mercyfull prince was there never: and to me he was ever a good, a gentle, and sovreigne lorde. And if any persone will medle of my cause, I require them to iudge the best. And thus I take my leve of the worlde and of you all, and I heartely desire you all to pray for me. O lorde have mercy on me, to God I comende my soule'.

As a special concession to the woman he had once loved, Henry had sent for a swordsman from Calais to carry out the execution. There was therefore no need of a block and Anne simply kneeled on the straw of the scaffold and said loudly 'to Christ I commend my soul'. The headsman did his job well and, with one blow of the sword, Anne's head was severed, her lips and eyes still moving in prayer as her head fell to the ground.

CHAPTER 18

Out of Hell Into Heaven

Anne's death caused shock waves across Europe and her guilt was widely believed. For the rest of Henry's reign and even during the reigns of his children, Anne remained despised and her entire life obliterated from history. As far as Henry and most of England were concerned, she had never been the king's wife and she had never been queen. As one contemporary wrote, following Henry's marriage to Jane Seymour which occurred only days after Anne's death, 'the king hath come out of hell into heaven, for the gentleness in this [Jane], and the cursedness and the unhappiness of the other [Anne]'. Traces of Anne's life were quickly erased, but she did leave a legacy.

As Norfolk had predicted before Anne's marriage, she was the ruin of her family. George, of course, died two days before Anne and his childless wife, Lady Rochford, followed them to the block in 1542. Thomas Boleyn was able to keep his rank as Earl of Wiltshire but, following the deaths of their children, both he and his wife retired from court for a time. They probably did so gladly, but Thomas, a career courtier, was unable to stay away from court for long and was back in favour by October 1537 when he played a prominent role at the christening of Edward, Henry's longed for son. Thomas must have looked at his own grandchild, Elizabeth, who was also present, and once again regretted that it was not his own daughter who had brought about this triumph. Elizabeth Howard is little recorded after Anne's fall and she probably kept away from the court. She remained a countess and she was given a grand funeral on 7 April 1538 as befitted her rank. Thomas Boleyn remained in favour after his wife's death and there were even rumours that he might marry the king's niece, Lady Margaret Douglas. Thomas never remarried and survived his wife by just over a year. He died a wealthy man but he cannot have been happy. Mary Boleyn, who had always been such a disappointment to her family, survived them as their sole heir and prudently spent the rest of her life in obscurity. She may not have been the grandest of the Boleyns, but she was almost certainly the happiest.

Following the deaths of Anne and George there was one further Boleyn survivor, and that was Anne's daughter, Elizabeth. Anne had always been a devoted mother to her only child and while in the Tower her thoughts must often have turned to her daughter. Anne knew that Elizabeth would suffer for her fall, as Mary had suffered when Catherine lost favour, but Anne must have hoped that Henry would, at least, provide for Elizabeth as his daughter. Shortly after Anne's death, parliament passed the Second Succession Act which declared Elizabeth a bastard and the lawful heirs the children of Jane Seymour. Elizabeth, in spite of her youth, also quickly felt her altered status. Soon after Anne's execution, Elizabeth's governess wrote to Cromwell begging for clothes for her young charge and stating that 'she hath neither gowns nor kirtle [slip], nor petticoat, nor no manner of linen nor rails [nightdress], nor body stichets [corsets], nor biggens [night caps]'. Elizabeth presumably received some clothing, but not in the manner to which she had been accustomed and not as Anne would have wanted. Although often neglected and ignored, Elizabeth survived her mother's fall and in spite of her illegitimacy Henry always acknowledged her as his child.

Elizabeth was a survivor and she will always be Anne Boleyn's greatest legacy. With the king's sixth marriage to Catherine Parr, Elizabeth was finally returned to the royal family and reinstated in the succession, even if she remained illegitimate at law. To Henry, at his death, Elizabeth seemed the least of his children but with the death of Catherine's daughter, Mary, in 1558, Elizabeth took the throne as perhaps the greatest ruler England ever had. Although Elizabeth never spoke publicly of Anne, she was kind to Anne's Howard relatives and the descendants of Mary Boleyn. More poignantly, on her death, a ring that Elizabeth always wore was found to contain a miniature portrait of the queen facing an image of her mother. This is a testament to Elizabeth's respect for her mother and Anne would have been proud of her daughter.

Elizabeth was not Anne's only legacy and the English Reformation will always be associated with her. At the time of her death, leading reformers desperately struggled to disassociate themselves from the fallen queen but in the reign of Elizabeth she was restored to her rightful place as one of the architects of the reformation. The reform movement assisted Anne in providing a solution to the king's divorce, but Anne's interest in the reform was genuine and committed. She was never the Protestant saint portrayed by William Latymer, John Foxe or Alexander Ales and she did not go to her death as a martyr. However, she was committed to the reform and she helped steer the king towards the break with Rome.

Anne's final legacy is one of which she would have been entirely unaware. Although Anne can never have realised, she was to be only the second wife of England's most married monarch. When Anne met Henry he had been married to Catherine of Aragon, a foreign princess, for many years and Henry's marital career was entirely conventional. Henry and Catherine had no son and, after Catherine's death he would have been expected to quickly remarry, perhaps to a French princess or another lady of the imperial family. Anne Boleyn changed all this. By insisting on marriage and driving Henry onwards, she broadened the king's horizons. Marriage to Anne showed Henry the possibility of choosing his own wife from amongst the noblewomen of his court. The marriage also showed other women, most notably Jane Seymour, the possibility of becoming a second Anne Boleyn. More pertinently, the break with Rome gave Henry the ability to rid himself of wives quickly and easily whenever he saw fit. Thanks to Anne, Henry never found himself married to another Catherine of Aragon clinging determinedly to her position. Instead Henry was able to change his wife whenever the mood suited him. This was the work of Anne Boleyn although she can never have expected or wanted it.

Anne Boleyn was the most vibrant and exceptional woman of her generation and she had the personality and drive to change history. She was no saint but neither was she a villain. Anne was simply very human. Anne Boleyn was extraordinary and her uniqueness fuelled a great obsession in Henry. Henry never knew another love like that which he felt for Anne and through his obsession he created an entirely unrealistic picture of his love. Even Anne Boleyn, as exceptional as she was, could not live up to this.

As Anne's enemy, Chapuys himself pointed out, Henry was very changeable and, as his obsession dimmed, Anne lost her ability to manage him. She was no victim and she fought until the end for her political survival. Although ultimately she lost the battle, Anne was the winner in the end. Among all of Henry's six wives, it is Anne who is remembered and it is Anne who changed England and left a truly lasting legacy. The price for Anne was high, but she would probably not have changed the course she decided upon back in 1527 when she first won Henry's love. Just as Mary Boleyn in her letter to Cromwell stated that she did not envy Anne as the greatest queen in Christendom, it is inconceivable that Anne would have envied her sister her quiet life. Anne Boleyn wanted to be a queen and she ensured that that is what she became. She would not have changed this even if she could have foreseen the future before her marriage to Henry.

Anne Boleyn was always Henry VIII's obsession and when he found that she could not live up to his high picture of her he brought her to her death. As Wolsey commented, the 'anger of the prince is death'. Anne was as well aware of this as her enemy the Cardinal. For Anne, it was a risk worth taking. Anne Boleyn was truly Henry VIII's obsession and when she failed to live up to this, his obsession turned to hatred. She was no helpless victim, she was a politician and she was the most exceptional woman of her time; a forerunner to her daughter, Elizabeth I.

Notes

Introduction

Denny 2004 provides a very sympathetic and almost unrecognisable saintly version of Anne. Chapman 1974 and Bruce 1972 also provide favourable accounts of Anne. Erickson 1980 gives a more hostile account. Ives 2005 is more detailed. Early accounts of Anne are contained in Benger 1821, Strickland 1844, Friedmann 1884, Round 1886 and Aiken 1818. Anne is also always the most prominent of Henry's queens in works on Henry VIII's six wives as a whole, such as Rival 1971, Fraser 2002, Weir 1991 and Starkey 2003.

Chapter 1: Sir Thomas Boleyn's Daughter

Round 1886:7 provides a summary of Anne's family background and her date of birth. Information on the Earl of Ormond, is contained in Sergeant 1923:2 and Round 1886:11. The rumours surrounding Elizabeth Howard are quoted from Sander 1877:23-24. The names of Anne's two brothers who died in infancy are taken from Dixon 1873:133. The details from the *Life of Jane Dormer* can be found in Clifford 1887:80. Gairdner 1895:104 considered that Anne's birth date was between 20 May and 31 December 1507. The relative seniority of Mary and Anne Boleyn is discussed in Round 1886 and Gairdner 1893. Lord Hunsdon's letter is quoted from Round 1886:18. The quotes concerning Anne's sixth finger and blemishes come from Wyatt 1825:183.

Chapter 2: So Pleasing in Her Youthful Age

Details of the life of Margaret of Austria can be found in

Hare 1907 and de Iongh 1954. Anne's stay in Brussels is noted in Paget 1981. The details of Margaret's repudiation are from Nedham 1979:121. Margaret's letter to her father is quoted from Hare 1907:208. Margaret's letter to Thomas Boleyn is from Sergeant 1923:12. Anne's letter is quoted from Sergeant 1923:17-18. Henry's imperial alliance and his French campaign are from Nedham 1979:121-122. Negotiations surrounding Mary Tudor's proposed marriage to Charles and the Dutch reaction to her French marriage are from Hall's Chronicle 1809:567-569. Mary Boleyn is included in the list of gentlewomen appointed to attend Mary in France (Brodie 1920, 3348). Mary Tudor's letter to her brother setting out their agreement is from Wood 1846:204. Anne's late arrival in France is suggested as only one 'Madamoyselle Boleyne' is included in a list of those ladies retained by the French king. Since both Mary and Anne Boleyn are known to have remained in France it seems likely that this is Mary rather than Anne who had still not yet arrived from Brussels (Brodie 1920:1414). Mary Tudor's relationship with Francis I comes from Brantome p368. Details of Mary Tudor's life can be found in Richardson 1970 and details of Suffolk's life can be found in Gunn 1988. Suffolk's promise not to marry Mary is contained in Brewer 1864:74. Suffolk's account of the marriage is contained in his letters to Wolsey dated 3 February 1515 and 5 March 1515 (Brewer 1864).

Chapter 3: Mademoiselle Boleyn

Details of Francis's licentiousness are from Brantome p9, 169 and 102. Sander's comments are from p26. Details of Claude's household are in Benger 1821. Sander 1877:26 claims Anne was a Lutheran. Details of the Field of the Cloth of Gold can be found in Russell 1969. The quote detailing Henry's rivalry with Francis is from Rawdon Brown, Four Years at the Court of Henry VIII, Letter II, 3 May 1515 (Williams 1967:390). The description of Henry from 1515 is also from Rawdon Brown, Letter I (Williams 1967:389). The description of the meeting of the two kings comes from Bodleian MS Ashmole 1116 (Russell 1969:210). The jousts and the banquets are described in Hall's Chronicle 1809:611 and 615. Details of the mass celebrated is in Bodleian MS Ashmole 1116 (Russell 1969:213). Bishop Fisher's comments on the Field of the Cloth of Gold are taken from his sermon (Russell 1969:216).

Chapter 4: A Secret Love

Anne's appearance is described in Wyatt 1825:182-183 and Sander 1877:25. The masque is described in Hall's Chronicle 1809:631. The ladies who played the virtues are listed in Brewer 1867:155. Details of the Butler marriage are in Round 1886:24, Dixon 1873:274, and Ives 2005:34-36. The reference to Anne's wilfulness comes from Wyatt 1968:143. The attraction between Anne and Henry Percy is detailed in Cavendish 1962:59-64. Information on Henry Percy is contained in Hoyle 1992. Anne's letter to Lady Wingfield is taken from Wood 1846:75. Wolsey's involvement in breaking Anne's engagement is in Cavendish 1962:59. Percy's letter to Cromwell is taken from Singer 1825:250.

Chapter 5: Fair Brunet

Wyatt's position at court and his love for Anne are contained in Wyatt 1825:184. Wyatt's poem referring to 'Brunet' can be found in Daalder 1975:90. Sander 1877:29 suggested that Anne was passionately in love with Wyatt. The extracts from the *Chronicle of Henry VIII* are from pp68-69. Harpsfield's account is from p253 and Sander's comments are from pp25, 28-29. George Wyatt's comments that if Thomas Wyatt had confessed it would have broken the marriage can be found in Wyatt 1968:183. The quote on Anne's chastity is taken from Wyatt 1825:194. Wyatt's poem on the hunt is in Daalder 1975:7. The quote concerning Anne's prominence at court comes from Wyatt 1968:185. The bowls game is described in Wyatt 1825:185. Thomson 1964:30 suggests Wyatt may have been out of favour with Henry.

Chapter 6: For Caesar's I Am

The quote about Anne not casting her eye on a married man comes from Wyatt 1825:194. Elizabeth Woodville's conduct is taken from More 2005:59. All Henry's letters to Anne are taken from Savage 1949. The first letter quoted concerning Henry's doubts is letter 1 (1949:28). Letter II is next quoted (1949:30). Letter3 enquires about Anne's health (1949:31-32). Anne Boleyn's letter to Henry is Letter 7 in Wood 1846. Henry's letter asking about Anne's feelings is letter 4 (1949:33-34). The claim that Anne loved Queen Catherine and was reluctant to marry Henry is in Wyatt 1825:188. Thomas Boleyn's reaction to Anne's engagement is from Wyatt 1825:187. Henry's letter concerning Anne's gift is letter 5 (1949:35-36). Henry's letter, desperate for Anne to return to court, is letter 11 (1949:42). The quote concerning Henry's desire to kiss Anne's breasts is from letter 16 (1949:47).

Chapter 7: The King's Great Matter

Catherine's marriage to Arthur is discussed in Wriothesley's Chronicle p5. Extracts from the *Life of Jane Dormer* are from p74. Anne and Catherine's card game is described in Wyatt 1825:188. Wolsey's attempts to secure an alliance with France are contained in Herbert 1649:215. Wolsey's attempts to obtain papal authority are in Hope 1894:53. The quote on the need for an embassy to Rome comes from a letter from Henry to Wolsey (St Clare Byrne 1968:48). Charles's determination to defend Catherine is taken from Herbert 1649:226. Anne's letter to Gardiner is from Brewer 1876:2382. Foxe's return to England is described in Foxe to Gardiner, 11 May 1528 (Brewer 1876:187). The description of the sweat is found in Du Bellay to Montmorency, 18 June 1528 (Brewer 1872:1924). Henry's letter to Anne during her illness is letter 12 (Savage 1949:44). Henry's happiness at Anne's recovery is found in Thomas Hennege to Wolsey, 23 June 1528 (Brewer 1872:1931). Henry's attempts to persuade Anne back to court are in letter 7 in Savage 1949:37. Henry's happiness at Anne's imminent return is found in letter 11 in Savage 1949:42. Henry's letter updating Anne on the legate's progress is letter 6 in Savage 1949:37. Anne's reluctance to meet the queen is documented in Du Bellay to Montmorency, 25 December 1528 (Brewer 1872:2207). Campeggio's attempts to negotiate with Henry and Catherine are from Herbert 1649:231. Campeggio's comments about Henry's intractability are found in Campeggio to Salviati, 28 October 1528 (St Clair Byrne 1968:86). Details of Arthur and Catherine's wedding night are found in Brewer 1876:2577. The instructions to Catherine regarding the brief are in Brewer 1876:2266. Catherine's speech can be found in Cavendish 1962:114-116. Campeggio's sentence and the uproar it caused are in the *Life of Fisher* p65-6.

Chapter 8: The Night Crow

Anne's letters to Wolsey are in Savage 1949:49-52. Henry's letter to Anne concerning Wilton is in Savage 1949:45. Isabel Jordan's letter to Wolsey is found in Wood 1846:37. Henry's two letters to Wolsey concerning Wilton are found in St

Clare Byrne 1968:77,79). The story concerning the banned book is from Wyatt 1825:203. The prophecy about Wolsey's destruction is in the *Chronicle of Henry VIII* p3. Anne's letter to Wolsey following Blackfriars is from Crawford 2002:188-189.Details of Anne's enmity towards Wolsey and her role in his fall are contained in Cavendish 1962. The quote speculating about Wolsey's refusal to submit to Henry Percy and details of Wolsey's death are from Herbert 1649:312-313.

Chapter 9: The Concubine

Details of Anne's fine lodging are contained in Du Bellay to Montmorency, 9 December 1528 (Brewer 1872:2177). Anne's disagreement with Norfolk is found in Chapuys to Charles V, 6 February 1530 (Brewer 1876:2781). The rumours that Norfolk had left court are from Augustine de Augustinis to the Duke of Norfolk, 3 June 1531 (Gairdner 1880:132). Anne's relationship with the Duchess of Norfolk is detailed in two letters from Chapuys to Charles V of 31 January and 14 May 1531 (Gairdner 1880:31 and 11). Anne's quarrel with her father is found in Chapuys to Granville, 11 July 1532 (Gairdner 1880:514). Anne's quarrel with Guildford is in Chapuys to Charles V, 6 June 1531 (Gairdner 1880:138). Anne's arguments with Henry are from Chapuys to Charles V, 27 November 1530 (Brewer 1876:3035), Mai to Francis de los Covos, 22 January 1531 (Gairdner 1880:27), Chapuys to Charles V, 29 April 1531 (Gairdner 1880:101) and Muxetula to Charles V, 23 January 1531 (Gairdner 1880:28). Anne's bravery is described in Chapuys to Charles V, 1 January 1531 (Gairdner 1880:10-11). Anne's partiality for York Place is noted in Chapuys to Charles V, 14 May 1531 (Gairdner 1880:110). The record of Henry and Catherine dining together is in Chapuys to Charles V, 14 May 1531 (Gairdner 1880:110). Catherine's response to Henry's abandonment of her is found in Chapuys to Charles V, 31 July 1531 (Gairdner 1880:167). Anne's hatred of Mary can be found in Chapuys to Charles V, 29 April 1531 (Gairdner 1880:101). Mary and Henry's meeting is recorded in Chapuys to Charles V, 1 October 1532 (Gairdner 1880:592). Anne's unpopularity is recorded in Du Bellay to Montmorency, 9 December 1528 (Brewer 1872:2177).The attempts made on Fisher's life can be found in the *Life of Fisher* p60-70 and Chapuys to Charles V, 1 March 1531 (Gairdner 1880:60). Anne and Henry's aborted hunting trip is chronicled in Chapuys to Charles V, 29 July 1532 (Gairdner 1880:526). Anne's appointment as Marchioness of Pembroke is described in Gairdner 1880:552. Anne and Henry's trip to France is detailed in Hall's Chronicle 1809:790-794. Anne's purchase of costly dresses and her appropriation of Catherine's jewels are found in Chapuys to Charles V, 1 October 1532 (Gairdner 1880:591). Attempts to find a French lady to meet Anne and Anne's comments about marrying in England are also noted in this source. The marriage is described in Harpsfield 1878:234 and Cranmer's letter to Archdeacon Hawkins, 17 June 1533 (Williams 1967:722).

Chapter 10: Pope in England

Hints dropped by Anne about her marriage are in Chapuys to Charles V, 15 February 1533 (Gairdner 1882:498). Henry's comments are taken from Chapuys to Charles V, 8 March 1533 (Gairdner 1882:97). Catherine's fears over Cranmer's appointment are found in Chapuys to Charles V, 9 February 1533 (Gairdner 1882:66). Chapuys's comment that Anne was a Lutheran comes from Chapuys to Charles V, 22 March 1531 (Gairdner 1882:69). Bernard (1993) also comments on the evidence for Anne's religious beliefs. Tyndale's words are from his preface to the New Testament in English (Bray 1994:19). Wyatt (1825:201-202) details that Anne was sent books by prominent reformers. Details of Simon Fish's *Supplication of the Beggars* can be found in Dowling 1984:36. Foxe (1965:58) comments on Anne's involvement in the reformation. Details of the praemunire manoeuvres can be found in Guy 1982 and Chapuys to Charles V, 14 February 1531 (Gairdner 1880:47). Lutheran preachers supported by Anne and her family are described in Chapuys to Charles V, 22 March 1531 and 13 May 1532 (Gairdner 1880). The Act for the Conditional Restraint of Annates can be found in Bray 1994:72. The comments from the *Life of Fisher* are from pp93-94. The despatch of the papal bulls confirming Cranmer's appointments are found in Chapuys to Charles V, 31 March 1533 (Gairdner 1882:127). The Act in Restraint of Appeals is from Bray 1994:79. Cranmer's account of the Dunstable court is found in Cranmer to Archdeacon Hawkyns, 17 June 1533 (Williams 1967:720). The Act of Supremacy is in Bray 1994:113-114. The quote from Wriothesley's Chronicle is from p30.

Chapter 11: The Most Happy

Anne's first appearance as queen is described in Chapuys to Charles V, 16 April 1533 (Gairdner 1882:168). Hostility towards Anne is described in John Coke, Secretary of the Merchant Adventurers, to Cromwell, 22 May 1533, John Coke, Clerk to the Merchant Adventurers at Antwerp to Cromwell, 30 June 1533, Examination of Sir Thomas Gebons, priest, and Sir Rauf Wendon, and Earl of Derby to Sir Henry Farryngton to Henry VIII, 10 August 1533 (Gairdner 1882:228,322,328 and 417). Henry's proclamation is from Chapuys to Charles V, 26 May 1533 (Gairdner 1882:235). Anne's seizure of Catherine's barge is noted in Chapuys to Charles V, 29 May 1533 (Gairdner 1882:244). Accounts of Anne's coronation are provided by Wynkyn de Worde (1903:11) and Chapuys to Charles V, 29 May 1533 (Gairdner 1882:244). The verses recited at the Leadenhall pageant are taken from Udall 1903:21. The hostile account of the coronation is taken from Gairdner 1882:266. The quote from the *Chronicle of Henry VIII* is p14. Cranmer's account of the coronation is contained in his letter to Archdeacon Hawkyns of 17 June 1533 (Williams 1967:720-721). Anne's coronation feast is recorded in Wriothesley's Chronicle p22. Sir Edward Baynton to Lord Rochford, 9 June 1533 (Gairdner 1882:282) provides details of the pastimes in Anne's chamber and Chapuys to Charles V, 28 June 1533 (Gairdner 1882:318) refers to the gift given to Anne by Francis I. Anne's demand for Catherine's christening robe is found in Chapuys to Charles V, 30 July 1533 (Gairdner 1882:397). Rumours of Henry's affair are found in Correspondence of Charles V, August 1533 (Gairdner 1882:446). The quote concerning Henry's mistress is found in Chapuys to Charles V, 3 September 1533 (Gairdner 1882:453). Henry's use of fortune tellers is in Chapuys to Charles V, 10 September 1533 (Gairdner 1882:465). Anne and Henry's reaction to Elizabeth's sex is found in Chapuys to Charles V, 10 September 1533 (Gairdner 1882:465). Rumours that Elizabeth would be named Mary are found in Chapuys to Charles V, 10 September 1533 (Gairdner 1882:465). An example of Anne's letters announcing the birth is her letter to Squire Josselin (Furnivall 1869:408-409). An account of Elizabeth's christening is contained in Hall's Chronicle 1809:805.

Chapter 12: Queen Anne

Elizabeth Barton's life is described in Cranmer to Archdeacon Hawkyns, 20 December 1533 (Gairdner 1882:624). There is also a detailed discussion in Bernard 2005. Barton's attempts to meet with Catherine are contained in Chapuys to Charles V,

12 November 1533 (Gairdner 1882:564). Barton's execution is in Wriothesley's Chronicle p24. George Boleyn's character is recorded in Cavendish 1825:20. George's purchase of hawks is recorded in his letter to Lord Lisle, 1533 (104) and Anthoine Brusset to Lord Lisle, 18 December 1533 (104a) (St Clare Byrne 1981:671). George's reformist views are discussed in Ives 1994. Anne's instructions to her chaplains are found in Latymer 1990:50. Anne's investigation of Hailes Abbey is found in Latymer 1990:61. Accounts of Anne's charity in Foxe are from p60. Freeman 1995 comments on the portrayal of Anne in Foxe. Anne's sponsorship of Mr Beckynsall is found in Latymer 1990:56. Anne's letter to the Abbot of St Mary's is found in Wood 1846:191-2. Anne's letter to Dr Crome is also found in Wood 1846:189. Anne's support of French exiles is detailed in Latymer 1990:56. Anne's support of Richard Herman is found in her letter to Cromwell (Gairdner 1883:255). The quote concerning Anne's virtues and mild nature comes from Foxe 1965:135. Anne's ambition for Elizabeth is found in Latymer 1990:63. Anne's devotion to Elizabeth is from the *Chronicle of Henry VIII* (p42). Elizabeth's procession to her own household is recorded in Chapuys to Charles V, 16 December 1533 (Gairdner 1882:617). Kingston's comments on Elizabeth are found in his letter to Lord Lisle, 18 April 1534 (169) (St Clare Byrne 1981:128). The first Act of Succession is found in Williams 1967:448. Henry's order that everyone should swear the oath of succession is in Wyatt 1825:205. The quote from Wriothesley's Chronicle is from p24.

Chapter 13: Rebels and Traitoresses

Lord Mountjoy's report is in Gairdner 1882:340. Attempts to move Catherine are contained within Chapuys to Charles V, 23 and 27 December 1533 (Gairdner 1882:629 and 633). Catherine's letter to Mary is taken from Gairdner 1882:472. The order regarding Mary's livery is found in Chapuys to Charles V, 15 September 1533 (Gairdner 1882:470). Mary's refusal to renounce her title is in Chapuys to Charles V, 10 October 1533 (Gairdner 1882:510). The announcement that Mary would be sent to join Elizabeth's household is taken from Chapuys to Charles V, 3 November 1533 (Gairdner 1882:556). Mary's comments about Elizabeth are found in Chapuys to Charles V, 23 December 1533 (Gairdner 1882:629). Henry's visit to Elizabeth is taken from Chapuys to Charles V, 17 January 1534 (Gairdner 1883:31). Anne's decision not to bring Mary to court is taken from Chapuys to Charles V, 29 January 1534 (Gairdner 1883:48). Anne's attempts to befriend Mary are recorded in Chapuys to Charles V, 7 March 1534 (Gairdner 1883:127). The incident in the *Life of Jane Dormer* is recorded on pp81-82. Anne's reference to Catherine and Mary as rebels and traiteresses is in Chapuys to Granvelle, 23 March 1536 (Gairdner 1883:169). Rumours that Anne intended to kill Mary are found in Chapuys to Charles V, 11 February and 23 June 1534 (Gairdner 1883:69 and 323). Mary Boleyn's letter is from Strickland 1844:231. George Taylor's letter to Lady Lisle of 27 April 1534 refers to Anne's pregnancy (St Clare Byrne 1981:139). A suggestion that this was a phantom pregnancy in Dewhurst 1984 seems unlikely given the recent birth of Elizabeth. Anne's instructions to George Boleyn to delay the French meeting are found in Gardiner 1883:366. Anne's confrontation with Henry is taken from Chapuys to Charles V, 27 September 1534 (Gairdner 1883:463). Anne's conspiracy with Lady Rochford is found in Chapuys to Charles V, 13 October 1534 (Gairdner 1883:485). Anne's outburst in front of the French ambassador is taken from Chapuys to Charles V, 14 January 1535 (De Gayangos 1886:376). The improvement in Mary's treatment is from Chapuys to Charles V, 24 October 1534 (Gairdner 1883:498). Anne's argument with Norfolk is found in Chapuys to Charles V, 1 January 1535 (Gairdner 1885:1). Anne's ability to manage the king is quoted from Chapuys to Charles V, 27 September 1534 (Gairdner 1883:463).

Chapter 14: No More Boys By Her

Fisher and More's imprisonment is detailed in Wriothesley's Chronicle p25. More's letter to Cromwell is from Gardiner 1883:123. Fisher's appointment as a cardinal is detailed in the *Life of Fisher* p111. Chapuys' visit to Catherine is included in Chapuys to Charles V, 9 January 1536 (Gairdner 1887:20-21). Chapuys' account of Catherine's death can be found in Chapuys to Charles V, 21 January 1536 (Gairdner 1887:49). Catherine's last letter is from Crawford 2002:179-180. Sander 1877:132 claims Henry wept on reading the letter and reports that Anne wore yellow in celebration. Henry's celebrations at Catherine's death are in Chapuys to Charles V, 21 January 1536 (Gairdner 1887:51). Chapuys' suspicions of poison are found in Chapuys to Charles V, 9 and 21 January 1536 (Gairdner 1887:22 and 51). Anne's attempts to befriend Mary are also found in Chapuys' dispatch of 21 January. Anne's letter to Lady Shelton is in Chapuys to Charles V, 17 February 1536

(Gairdner 1887:117-118). Details of Catherine's funeral can be found in Gardiner 1887:14. Anne's miscarriage is noted in Chapuys to Charles V, 10 February 1536 (Gairdner 1887:102). Henry's anger towards Anne is chronicled in Wyatt 1825:208. Henry's claim that Anne had bewitched him is found in Chapuys to Charles V, 29 January 1536 (Gairdner 1887:70). Anne's attempts to blame Norfolk are found in Chapuys to Charles V, 10 February 1536 (Gairdner 1887:102). Henry's affair with Jane Seymour is described in Wyatt 1825:208 and Sander 1877:132. Anne's claim that Henry had broken her heart is contained in Chapuys to Charles V, 25 February 1536 (Gairdner 1887:134).

Chapter 15: Sick and Tired of the Concubine

Claims that Henry was barely speaking to Anne are in Chapuys to Charles V, 25 February 1536 (Gairdner 1887:134). Details about Jane Seymour are in Seymour 1972 and Gross 1999. Jane's refusal of Henry's gift and his increasing affection for her is detailed in Chapuys to Charles V, 1 April 1536 (Gairdner 1887:245). Henry's letter to Jane is in Savage 1949:69. The coaching Jane received is described in Chapuys to Charles V, 1 April 1536 (Gairdner 1887:245). Anne's rage at Jane is documented in Chapuys to Granvelle, 18 March 1536 (Gairdner 1887:202). Chapuys' support for Jane is contained in Chapuys to Charles V, 1 April 1536 (Gairdner 1887:245). Ales' account can be found on p526. Chapuys' discussion with Cromwell is in Chapuys to Charles V, 1 April 1536 (Gairdner 1887:243-245). Charles V's instructions to Chapuys of 28 March 1536 are in Gairdner 1887:275. Chapuys' recognition of Anne is in Chapuys to Charles V, 21 April 1536 (Gairdner 1887:290). Sander 1877:132 claims that Anne's child was deformed. Anne's failure to secure an appointment as a knight of the garter for George Boleyn is noted in Chapuys to Charles V, 29 April 1536 (Gairdner 1887:315). Anne's appeal to Henry with Elizabeth is recorded in Ales 1863:527. Chapuys' comment that Henry was sick of Anne is in Chapuys to Charles V, 29 April 1536 (Gairdner 1887:315). There are a number of theories for the fall of Anne Boleyn and why it happened so rapidly. Walker 2002 considers that the commission was not set up specifically for Anne and was merely used as a convenient instrument when the scandal concerning Anne broke. Bernard 1991 and 1992 considers that Henry had grounds for suspicion towards Anne and that there was evidence for her guilt. Ives 1992 and 2005 counters this view and considers that Cromwell actively worked to destroy Anne. More unusually, Warnicke 1985 considers that a number of court factions grouped together behind Jane Seymour to oppose Anne. Warnicke 1989 holds the view that Anne gave birth to a deformed foetus which raised accusations of incest. In reality, Anne was probably brought down by the king falling in love with another woman and court faction.

Chapter 16: Turned Trust to Treason

Smeaton's arrest and Henry's interrogation of Norris can be found in Constantine 1831:64. Sander 1877:133 records the dropped handkerchief. Henry's sudden departure from the jousts is recorded in Hall's Chronicle 1809:819. Lady Wingfield's deathbed statement is discussed in Warnicke 1989:120. John Husee's letter to Lady Lisle is in St Clare Byrne 1981:378. Lady Worcester's letter to Cromwell of 8 March 1537 is in Wood 1846:319. Lady Worcester's accusation is discussed in Walker 2002:17. Ales 1863:527 states that spies were placed in Anne's household. Lady Rochford's malice is discussed in Wyatt 1825:212. Anne's arrest is detailed in Wriothesley's Chronicle p36. Herbert 1649:382 details Anne's request to see the king. Anne's arrival at the Tower is described in Wriothesley's Chronicle p36. Anne's conversation with William Kingston on her arrival and first days in the Tower are contained in Kingston to Cromwell, letter I (in Singer 1825:217-220). Anne's mention of Smeaton in the Tower is in Kingston to Cromwell, letter II (in Singer 1825:222). Anne's words concerning her brother are in the same letter. Details of Brereton's life can be found in Ives 1976. Constantine's comments regarding Brereton are on pp64-65. Anne's comments that she was cruelly handled are in Kingston to Cromwell, letter III (in Singer 1825:224). Cranmer's letter to Henry is in Strickland 1844:250-251. Cranmer's comments to Ales on Anne's death are contained in Ales p528. Jane Dormer's belief in Anne's guilt is included in Clifford 1887:79. Comments about Anne's guilt in the *Chronicle of Henry VIII* are on pages 55 and 59. Chapuys' comments about Anne's guilt are in Chapuys to Charles V, 2 May 1536 (Gairdner 1887:330). Cromwell's letter to Gardiner and Wallop of 14 May 1563 is in Gairdner 1887:360. Henry's comments to the Duke of Richmond are in Chapuys to Charles V, 19 May 1536 (Gairdner 1887:377). Ales' comments on Anne's guilt are on p569. Cavendish 1825:40 contains the reference about turning trust to treason.

Chapter 17: The Lady in the Tower

The men's trial is detailed in the reports of Sir John Spelman (1977:71). The anonymous account of Anne's trial is contained in Harl. MS. 2194, Leaf 16 (Furnivall 1869:229). Henry Percy's illness is noted in Gairdner 1887:363. Wriothesley's Chronicle also provides an account of Anne's trial on p37. Sir John Spelman's record of the offences Anne was charged with are on p71. The list of charges against Anne can be found in Gairdner 1887:362-363. The reference to Norfolk's tears are in Constantine 1831:66. Chapuys provides an account of George's trial in Chapuys to Charles V, 19 May 1536 (Gairdner 1887:378). Chapuys' account of Henry's impotence is contained in Chapuys to Antoine Perrenot, 18 May 1536 (Gairdner 1887:324). Cromwell's assurance to Sir Henry Wyatt is noted in Muir 1963:30. Speculation over the fate of Wyatt and Page is contained in John Husee to Lady Lisle on 12 and 13 May 1536 (letters 694 and 695) (in St Clair Byrne 1981). Anne's last letter to Henry is taken from Crawford 2002:193-194. Details of the annulment of Anne's marriage come from Wriothesley's Chronicle p41. George Boleyn's speech is taken from the *Chronicle of Calais* (Nichols 1846:46). The other speeches are taken from Constantine (1831). Anne's words on Smeaton's death are from Gairdner 1887:431. Comments about Anne's declaration of innocence are taken from Kingston to Cromwell, 18 May 1536, letter VI (in Singer 1825:229) and Chapuys to Charles V, 19 May 1536 (Gairdner 1887:380). Anne's comments about a possible nickname come from Chapuys to Granvelle, 6 June 1536 (Gairdner 1887:453). Anne's scaffold speech is recorded in a number of sources with slight variations. The version used here is from Hall's Chronicle 1809:819. The account of Anne's last few moments is taken from Spelman (1977:59).

Chapter 18: Out of Heaven Into Hell

The quote comparing Anne and Jane is from Sir John Russell to Lord Lisle, 3 June 1536 (St Clare Byrne 1981:396). Anne's sister-in-law, Lady Rochford, was executed with Henry's fifth wife, Catherine Howard, for assisting in that queen's adultery. An account of Elizabeth Howard's funeral is contained in John Husee to Lady Lisle, 9 April 1538 (St Clare Byrne 1981:99). Rumours that Thomas Boleyn was to marry Henry's niece are found in Henry Monk to Lady Lisle, 19 July 1538 (St Clare Byrne 1981:184). Extracts from the Second Succession

Act can be found in Williams 1967:452. Elizabeth's governess, Lady Bryan's letter to Cromwell is taken from Falkus 1974:88. Wolsey's comment is from Cavendish 1962:177.

Bibliography

Primary Sources

Ales, A., 'Alexander Ales to the Queen, 1 September 1559' in Stevenson, J. (ed.), *Calendar of State Papers, Foreign Series, of the Reign of Elizabeth, 1558-1559* (London, 1863)

Bayne, R. (ed.), *The Life of Fisher* (London, 1921)

Brantome, the Seigneur de, *Lives of Fair and Gallant Ladies* (London, undated)

Bray, G. (ed.), *Documents of the English Reformation* (Cambridge, 1994)

Brewer, J.S. (ed.), *Letters and Papers, Foreign and Domestic of the Reign of Henry VIII, vol II* (London, 1864)

Letters and Papers, Foreign and Domestic of the Reign of Henry VIII, vol III (London, 1867)

Letters and Papers, Foreign and Domestic of the Reign of Henry VIII, vol IV (London, 1872)

Letters and Papers, Foreign and Domestic of the Reign of Henry VIII, vol IV (London, 1876)

Brodie, R.H. (ed.), *Letters and Papers, Foreign and Domestic of the Reign of Henry VIII, vol I* (London, 1920)

Cavendish, G., 'Metrical Visions', in Singer, S.W. (ed.), *The Life of Cardinal Wolsey* (Chiswick, 1825)

Thomas Wolsey Late Cardinal, His Life and Death, ed. Lockyer, R. (London, 1962)

Clifford, H., *The Life of Jane Dormer Duchess of Feria*, ed. Estcourt, E.E. and Stevenson (London, 1887)

Constantine, G., *Transcript of an Original Manuscript, Containing a Memorial from George Constantyne to Thomas Lord Cromwell*, ed. Amyot, T.(Archaeologia 23, 1831)

Crawford, A., *Letters of the Queens of England* (Stroud, 2002)

Falkus, C. (ed.), *The Private Lives of the Tudor Monarchs* (London, 1974)

Foxe, J., *The Acts and Monuments*, ed. Townsend, G. (New York, 1965)

Furnivall, Mr, (ed.) *Ballad Society, First Report* (London, 1869)

Gairdner, J., (ed.) *Letters and Papers, Foreign and Domestic of the Reign of Henry VIII, vol V* (London, 1880)

Letters and Papers, Foreign and Domestic of the Reign of Henry VIII, vol VI (London, 1882)

Letters and Papers, Foreign and Domestic of the Reign of Henry VIII, vol VII (London, 1883)

Letters and Papers, Foreign and Domestic of the Reign of Henry VIII, Vol VIII (London, 1885)

Letters and Papers, Foreign and Domestic of the Reign of Henry VIII, vol X (London, 1887)

Guangos, P., de (ed.), *Calendar of Letters, Despatches, and State Papers, Relating to the Negotiations Between England and Spain, vol V, pt I* (London, 1886)

Hall, E., *Hall's Chronicle Containing the History of England During the Reign of Henry IV and the Succeeding Monarchs to the End of the Reign of Henry VIII* (London, 1809)

Harpsfield, N., *A Treatise on the Pretended Divorce Between Henry VIII and Catherine of Aragon* (London, 1878)

Herbert, E., *The Life and Raigne of King Henry the Eighth* (London, 1649)

Hume, M.A.S, *Chronicle of King Henry VIII* (London, 1889)

Latymer, W., *Chronickille of Anne Bulleyne,* ed. Dowling, M. (Camden Miscellany XXX, Fourth Series, Vol 39, 1990)

More, T., *The History of King Richard III* (London, 2005)

Nedham, G., *The Politics of a Tudor Merchant Adventurer: A Letter to the Earls of Friesland,* ed. Ramsay, G.D. (Manchester, 1979)

Nichols, J.G. (ed.), *The Chronicle of Calais* (London, 1846)

Sander, N., *Rise and Growth of the Anglican Schism* (London, 1877)

Savage, H., *The Love Letters of Henry VIII* (London, 1949)

Singer, S.W. (ed.), *The Life of Cardinal Wolsey by William Cavendish* (Chiswick, 1825)

Spelman, J., *The Reports of Sir John Spelman,* ed. Baker, J.H. (London, 1977)

St Clare Byrne, M. (ed.), *The Letters of King Henry VIII* (London, 1968)

The Lisle Letters (Chicago, 1981)

Udall, N., 'English Verses and Ditties at the Coronation Procession of Queen Anne Boleyn' in Pollard, A.F. (ed.), *Tudor Tracts* (Westminster, 1903)

Williams, C.H., *English Historical Documents, vol V* (London, 1967)

Wood, M.A.E. (ed.), *Letters of Royal and Illustrious Ladies* (London, 1846)

Worde, W. De, 'The Manner of the Triumph at Calais and Boulogne' and 'The Noble and Triumphant Coronation of Queen Anne' in Pollard, A.F. (ed.) *Tudor Tracts* (Westminster, 1903)

Wriothesley, C., *A Chronicle of England During the Reigns of the Tudors,* ed. Hamilton, W.D. (London, 1875)

Wyatt, G., 'Extracts from the Life of the Virtuous Christian and Renowned Queen Anne Boleigne', in Singer, S.W. (ed.), *The Life of Cardinal Wolsey* (Chiswick, 1825)

The Papers of George Wyatt Esquire, ed. Loades, D.M. (London, 1968)

Wyatt, T., *Collected Poems,* ed. Daalder, J. (London, 1975)

Bibliography

Secondary Sources

Aiken, L., *Memoirs of the Court of Queen Elizabeth* (London, 1818)

Benger, E.O., *Memoirs of the Life of Anne Boleyn*, 2 vols (London, 1821)

Bernard, G.W., *The Fall of Anne Boleyn* (English Historical Review 106, 1991)

The Fall of Anne Boleyn: A Rejoinder (English Historical Review 107, 1992)

Anne Boleyn's Religion (The Historical Journal 36, 1993)

The King's Reformation (London, 2005)

Bruce, M.L., *Anne Boleyn* (London, 1972)

Chapman, H.W., *Anne Boleyn* (London, 1974)

Denny, J., *Anne Boleyn* (London, 2004)

Dewhurst, J., *The Alleged Miscarriages of Catherine of Aragon and Anne Boleyn* (Medical History 28, 1984)

Dixon, W.H., *History of Two Queens* (London, 1873)

Dowling, M., *Anne Boleyn and Reform* (Journal of Ecclesiastical History 35, 1984)

Erickson, C., *Anne Boleyn* (London, 1984)

Fraser, A., *The Six Wives of Henry VIII* (London, 2002)

Freeman, T.S., *Research, Rumour and Propaganda: Anne Boleyn in Foxe's 'Book of Martyrs'* (The Historical Journal 38, 1995)

Friedmann, P., *Anne Boleyn* (London, 1884)

Gairdner, J., *Mary and Anne Boleyn* (English Historical Review 8, 1893)

The Age of Anne Boleyn (English Historical Review 10, 1895)

Gross, P., *Jane the Quene* (Lewiston, 1999)

Gunn, S.J., *Charles Brandon, Duke of Suffolk* (Oxford, 1988)

Guy, J.A., *Henry VIII and the Praemunire Manoeuvres of 1530-1531* (English Historical Review 97, 1982)

Hare, C., *The High and Puissant Princess Marguerite of Austria* (London, 1907)

Hope, Mrs, *The First Divorce of Henry VIII* (London, 1894)

Hoyle, R.W., Henry Percy, Sixth Earl of Northumberland, and the Fall of the House of Percy, in Bernard, G.W. (ed.), *The Tudor Nobility* (Manchester, 1992)

Iongh, J., de, *Margaret of Austria* (London, 1954)

Ives, E.W., *Letters and Accounts of William Brereton of Malpas* (The Record Society of Lancashire and Cheshire 106, 1976)

The Fall of Anne Boleyn Reconsidered (English Historical Review 107, 1992)

Anne Boleyn and the Early Reformation in England: The Contemporary Evidence (The Historical Journal 37, 1994)

The Life and Death of Anne Boleyn (Oxford, 2005)

Muir, K., *The Life and Letters of Sir Thomas Wyatt* (Liverpool, 1963)

Norton. E., *She Wolves: The Notorious Queens of England* (Stroud, 2008)

Paget, H., *The Youth of Anne Boleyn* (Bulletin of the Institute of Historical Research 54, 1981)

Richardson, W.C., *Mary Tudor: The White Queen* (London, 1970)

Rival, P., *The Six Wives of King Henry VIII* (London, 1971)

Round, J.H., *The Early Life of Anne Boleyn* (London, 1886)

Russell, J.G., *The Field of the Cloth of Gold* (London, 1969)

Sergeant, P.W., *The Life of Anne Boleyn* (London, 1923)

Seymour, W., *Ordeal by Ambition* (London, 1972)

Starkey, D., *Six Wives* (London, 2003)

Strickland, A., *Lives of the Queens of England, vol IV* (London, 1844)

Thomson, P., *Sir Thomas Wyatt and His Background* (London 1964)

Walker, G., *Rethinking the Fall of Anne Boleyn* (The Historical Journal 45, 2002)

Warnicke, R.M., *The Fall of Anne Boleyn: A Reassessment* (History 70, 1985)

The Rise and Fall of Anne Boleyn (Cambridge, 1989)

Weir, A., *The Six Wives of Henry VIII* (London, 1991)

List of Illustrations

26. The chapel of St Peter ad Vincula. (Elizabeth Norton).
27. Anne Boleyn. (Elizabeth Norton).
28. A later artist's impression of Anne Boleyn. (Elizabeth Norton).
29. Anne's father, Thomas Boleyn. (Elizabeth Norton).
30. Anne's uncle, the Duke of Norfolk. (Elizabeth Norton).
31. Margaret of Austria. (Elizabeth Norton).
32. Mary Tudor, the French Queen. (Elizabeth Norton).
33. Francis I of France. (Elizabeth Norton).
34. Henry VIII. (Elizabeth Norton).
35. Thomas Wyatt. (Elizabeth Norton).
36. Cardinal Wolsey. (Elizabeth Norton).
37. Catherine of Aragon. (Elizabeth Norton).
38. Emperor Charles V. (Elizabeth Norton).
39. Pope Clement VII. (Elizabeth Norton).
40. William Warham. (Elizabeth Norton).
41. Thomas Cranmer. (Elizabeth Norton).
42. Thomas Cromwell. (Elizabeth Norton).
43. Anne's daughter, Elizabeth I as queen. (Elizabeth Norton).
44. Mary Tudor. (Elizabeth Norton).
45. Thomas More. (Elizabeth Norton).
46. Jane Seymour. (Elizabeth Norton).
47. A nineteenth century illustration of the condemnation of Anne Boleyn. (Elizabeth Norton).
48. A nineteenth century representation of the execution of Anne Boleyn. © Jonathan Reeve JR965b20p921 15001600.
49. A nineteenth century representation of Henry VIII and Anne Boleyn. © Jonathan Reeve JR959b61p689 15001600.
50. A distant prospect of Greenwich Palace. © Jonathan Reeve JR944b46fp180 14501500.
51. London in *c.* 1600. (Stephen Porter and the Amberley Archive).
52. Letter from Anne Boleyn to Stephen Gardiner. © Jonathan Reeve JR964b20p900 15001600.
53. One of a series of friendly letters which Anne Boleyn wrote to Cardinal Wolsey. © Jonathan Reeve JR963b20p899 15001600.
54. An Anonymous drawing of Henry VIII. © Jonathan Reeve JR951b53p505 15001550.
55. Ripon Cathedral portrait of Anne Boleyn. (The Chapter, Ripon Cathedral.

INDEX

Tudor History from Amberley Publishing

THE TUDORS
Richard Rex

'The best introduction to England's most important dynasty'
DAVID STARKEY
'Gripping and told with enviable narrative skill... a delight'
THES
'Vivid, entertaining and carrying its learning lightly'
EAMON DUFFY
'A lively overview' **THE GUARDIAN**
£16.99   978-1-84868-049-4   320 pages (100 colour illus)

CATHERINE HOWARD
Lacey Baldwin Smith

'Lacey Baldwin Smith is one of our finest historians' **ALISON WEIR**
'A faultless book' **THE SPECTATOR**
'Lacey Baldwin Smith has so excellently caught the
atmosphere of the Tudor age' **THE OBSERVER**
£20.00   978-1-84868-214-6   240 pages (25 colour illus)

MARGARET OF YORK
Christine Weightman

'A pioneering biography of the Tudor dynasty's most
dangerous enemy'
PROFESSOR MICHAEL HICKS
'Christine Weightman brings Margaret alive once more'
THE YORKSHIRE POST
'A fascinating account of a remarkable woman'
THE BIRMINGHAM POST
£14.99   978-1-84868-099-9   208 pages (40 illus)

THE SIX WIVES OF HENRY VIII
David Loades

'Neither Starkey nor Weir has the assurance and command
of Loades'
SIMON HEFFER, LITERARY REVIEW
£14.99   978-1-84868-335-8   240 pages (40 colour illu

ANNE BOLEYN
Elizabeth Norton

£9.99   978-1-84868-514-7
264 pages (47 illus, 26 colour)

MARY BOLEYN
Josephine Wilkinson

£18.99   978-1-84868-089-0
240 pages (22 illus, 10 colour)

JANE SEYMOUR
Elizabeth Norton

£20.00   978-1-84868-102-6
240 pages (53 illus, 26 colour)

THE EARLY LOVES OI
ANNE BOLEYN
Josephine Wilkinson
£20.00   978-1-84868-430-0
288 pages (30 colour illus)

ANNE OF CLEVES
Elizabeth Norton

£20.00   978-1-84868-329-7
288 pages (55 illus, 20 colour)

HENRY VIII
Richard Rex

£9.99   978-1-84868-098-2
240 pages (60 illus, 20 colour)

ELIZABETH I
Richard Rex

£9.99   978-1-84868-423-2
192 pages (76 illus)

Available from all good bookshops or to order direct
Please call **01285-760-030**
www.amberley-books.com

About the Author

Elizabeth Norton gained her first degree from the University of Cambridge, and her Masters from the University of Oxford. Her other books include *Jane Seymour: Henry VIII's True Love*, *Anne of Cleves: Henry VIII's Discarded Bride* (both published by Amberley Publishing) and *She Wolves: The Notorious Queens of England*. She lives in Kingston Upon Thames.

Also by Elizabeth Norton: